Tales of
SULLOM WOE

Tales of
SULLOM WOE

Bill Jardine

The Pentland Press
Edinburgh • Cambridge • Durham

First published in 1993 by
The Pentland Press Ltd.
1 Hutton Close
South Church
Bishop Auckland
Durham

ISBN 1 85821 091 7

Typeset by CBS, Felixstowe, Suffolk
Printed and bound by Antony Rowe Ltd., Chippenham

PREFACE

This tale was prompted by Doctor Jonathan Wills, author and lately editor of that august journal, *The Shetland Times*, who suggested during a visit to his schloss on Bressay that twelve years working at Sullom Voe should have provided enough material to write a book.

It seemed, as Brutus said after he stuck it into Caesar, like a good idea at the time.

As the tale developed, however, it soon became apparent that certain members of the Corporate Hierarchy of that munificent oil company which will hopefully be funding my pension might not be over enamoured with the prospect of their minor slips being exposed in print. To save any embarrassment – the prospect of libel suits never entered my head – I have changed the names of the characters; all of them, however, do exist, and will be readily recognised by their fellow veterans.

Similarly, my ex-wife is less than charitably portrayed, as those who know her will readily agree; the portrayal of her as a sort of female Quasimodo is highly fictionalised, but was essential to the plot.

The story is roughly chronological, and covers the period from 1978 to 1990. It is not about life on an oil terminal, but about people, and could, in fact, have been set in any work environment.

Good books are usually dedicated, and I can't see any reason why bad books should be any different.

I therefore dedicate this book to all those who appear within its pages, and are therefore responsible for its existence.

My thanks are due to Jonathan Wills, Nigel Martin, aspiring Clark Kent and chief snooper of the *Sullom Voe Scene*, and last but not least, my current wife Adrienne, better known as The Grunt.

PROLOGUE

1977 had not been a good year; I had spent most of it away from home, which was, in retrospect, the best part, since constant domestic reruns of World War Two, with even more gratuitous violence than the prototype, were pretty well the only memorable episodes in my mark one marriage.

In the spring of the year I had taken myself off to sea or, more specifically, found myself a job on an ancient paddle-steamer transporting up and down the Clyde those demented souls who consider that the next best thing to walking on water is sailing upon it.

Sailing is a remarkably hazardous occupation, especially for those who, like myself, are foolhardy enough to sign on as cooks, while lacking sufficient culinary ability to boil an egg.

The risks were further heightened by the fact that most of the recipients of my efforts were residents of Culture City, who are less inclined to use their heads to work out the intricacies of *The Times* crossword than as a means of inflicting grievous bodily harm.

It soon became obvious to me that returning to sea was not a good career move. At that time my mother resided in Glasgow, and I frequently stayed there during the ship's overnight stops, since the vessel's crew accommodation bore more than a passing resemblance to the hold of an eighteenth century slaver.

My fond parent – who had observed the bandages which concealed the plaudits heaped upon her offspring by his appreciative patrons – had instinctively known that all was not well. One evening she produced a copy of a newspaper which contained a recruitment advertisement for a new oil terminal at Sullom Voe. She read the advertisement out to me;

the advertiser was looking for a variety of highly skilled and technologically orientated personnel to man this new operation.

On the face of it an "O" Level in food cremation didn't really seem an appropriate qualification, but it seemed logical that working on an oil terminal in a state of blissful ignorance was a damn sight safer than trying to pass off burnt mince as a culinary feast to hundreds of highly unpredictable Glasgwegian aboriginals.

The advertisement failed to expand on the location of this technological Shangri-la, but my parent had a distant relative who had spent the war chasing the Italians across North Africa, and being chased in his turn by the Afrika Korps.

Having listened to his tales of blood and slaughter over the ensuing quarter of a century, Mother seemed to recollect that Sullom was a minor sheikdom somewhere between Libya and Morocco. This seemed a reasonable supposition, since it didn't appear on the comprehensive map of the British Isles in the back of my diary. I cut out the application form and stuck it in the back of my wallet in case of emergency.

The River Clyde is reckoned to have within its shores some of the safest sailing waters in the world; there are few currents, no pirates (apart from the ferry company), no typhoons, and no uncharted reefs. Despite the almost total lack of natural hazards, the captain of my ship managed to put his command ashore on virtually the only rock of consequence in the river, in broad daylight and in full view of literally thousands of spectators, and suffered the crushing indignity of having his vessel rescued by the United States Navy.

Never mind women and children first – I was in such a hurry to get into a lifeboat that I forgot to burn the mince.

It seemed to me that the emergency for which I had saved the advertisement had arrived; plots were afoot to sail the ship to exotic places like Llandudno and London, and there were a lot of rocks on the route.

Spurred on by an overriding sense of self preservation, I wrote off for the job, having convinced myself that, despite the rather unstable geopolitical status of the Middle East, it beat having my last resting place marked by a wreck buoy, or having an irate gourmet perform an appendectomy on me with the soup ladle.

A few weeks later, while sampling the exotic delights of a foreign port – the Fort Bar in Ayr, to be precise – I fell into the company of fellow inebriates and happened to mention Sullom Voe.

In the corner there was slumped an apparition who had obviously spent his evening trying to embalm himself in alcohol. At the mention of Sullom Voe, his eyelids creaked open and he fixed me with a set of eyes which had undoubtedly originated in a Golden Wonder potato.

"Ah've jist come frae therr," he slurred, "an' ah'm no' goin' back. Ah only went tae get away frae the wife; she's like a Dobermann wi' tits an' she's made ma life hell fur fifteen years. But ah'll tell ye this, efter three weeks up therr this place is paradise an' she's Bo Derek."

I gathered from his drift that he was less than enamoured with Sullom Voe; however, his reference to "up therr" I found puzzling, since North Africa is unquestionably down rather than up.

The seeds of doubt were beginning to form in my mind and it also struck me that, if he had spent three weeks in North Africa, he shouldn't have the colour euphemistically known in the underworld as a Peterheid Suntan.

My informant, however, was now in full flood.

"Aboot two inches doon frae the Arctic Circle," he expanded."Nae trees, nae pubs, hunnerd mile an oor winds an' nuthin but mud everywhere. Nae wimmen, jist sheep...mind ye," he mused reflectively, " ah could huv got used tae that."

At that point the conversation terminated; the narrator yawned a large quantity of Messrs Tennents Patent Embalming Fluid and diced carrots on to the floor and collapsed abruptly into his corner.

It seemed my grasp of geography was a little awry, and a little homework on the location of Sullom Voe revealed that it was concealed in a little box at the top end of the map of Britain. The reason for the box puzzled me (I was later to discover that a favourite Shetland T- shirt logo is a full size map of Shetland with Britain in a little box at the bottom) until I found out to my consternation that it was too far away to fit into the map.

Some time, however, had elapsed without any response to my application, and it seemed that I had escaped the fate outlined by my erstwhile drinking companion.

Somewhere at sea, however, things were getting decidedly sticky; when I made a rash venture into exotica with bread and butter pudding, the crew's appreciation of my culinary efforts reached homicidal levels.

Black Spots were coming through the galley door like confetti, and I took to sleeping in the funnel out of harm's way. I telephoned home in a blind panic and informed my nearest and dearest that the sailor was coming home from the sea. If I was to be beaten to a pulp by some pea-brained titan with murder on its mind, I'd sooner it was done by the wife.

The British Merchant Navy has sunk to miniscule proportions in the last few years; shipping companies can afford to be choosy. There are few who will take on men whose sole qualification is the production of fifty-seven different varieties of salmonella. My wife, however, managed to find one, and phoned me with the news that she had procured for me a berth as a deckhand on a coaster, presently lying at Stranraer.

"What's she called?" I asked.

"Dunno," she grunted (she was good at grunting – she had the face for it).

"Where's it going?" I enquired further.

"Will ye stoap askin' stupid questions an' get doon tae Stranraer!" she snarled. "Ah goat ye the joab – whit mair dae ye want?"

Since she was paying for the call I thought it diplomatic not to answer, although a fairly lengthy wish list came to mind, starting with divorce and running through a whole gamut of dream scenarios which culminated in a fairly conclusive encounter between my wife and a runaway bus.

The next day saw me wandering around Stranraer searching for my new ship. Stranraer is definitely not high on my list of exotic ports; a bit like Murmansk without the glamour. Perched forlornly in a corner of the harbour was a rust-streaked hulk which had obviously slipped through the net when Lloyds were dishing out seaworthiness certificates. I carefully checked the label on the sharp end, which read *"Raylight"*, and established that this was indeed the vessel I was looking for.

I made my way aboard and was greeted by the engineer, who was called Jimmy, and spoke in that strange brand of pseudo-English which identified him as one of that tribe of aboriginals which had dogged my chequered career in my previous berth.

"Where are we going?" said I.

"God knows," said he, "an' he's doon below waitin' fur ye tae come aboard an' sign oan." God, better known as Big Tam, was indeed awaiting my arrival, and was perched on a chair in his day cabin, glaring at me like a malevolent buddha. "Aboot time ye goat here. Get yersel' signed oan an' get up oan deck wi' the rest...we're aff."

I made my way topside, thinking that the skipper wasn't exactly the most sociable person I'd met, and he hadn't even tasted my cooking.

On deck I met the rest of the crew, the bosun and the other deckhand.

It occurred to me that one of my fellow seafarers might have some knowledge of our destination. As we were casting off, I decided to ask the bosun.

"Where are we bound?" I enquired.

"Ah'm no' quite sure," he said, uncertainly, "Ah've never heard of the place, but ah think it's somewhere in North Africa."

A bell thundered in my head like the crack of doom. "It's not Sullom Voe, is it?" I asked.

"That's the place!" he said brightly, waving enthusiastically to a passing seagull, which treated his greeting with undisguised contempt.

This confirmed that, not only were we bound for the place so graphically described as hell on earth by my acquaintance of a short time ago, but that I was to share the passage with a crew who might be more appropriately clad in strait-jackets.

The passage was not a fun experience; my relationship with the skipper, with whom I had to share wheel watches, was fraught to say the least. It didn't need burnt mince to turn Big Tam homicidal, and the word paranoia was invented to describe his demeanour.

He was a devout megalomaniac and vented his spleen on the hapless engineer, who spent the voyage in self-imposed exile in the engine-room to escape the skipper's wrath.

At length we arrived in Shetland, and dropped anchor in Sullom Voe, joining a queue of other vessels awaiting berths.

We lay off for a week and had plenty of time to soak up the ambience. The view was not inspiring. The only activity ashore seemed to consist of a constant stream of huge trucks engaged in carrying vast quantities of mud backwards and forwards; a multitude of small figures clad in green oilskins scuttled about the wasteland like demented ants with no apparent purpose.

There were no trees, no sign of normal human habitation, nothing remotely resembling a woman, and, even after five days at sea and a week at anchor, the few dejected sheep on the moonscape aroused not the slightest stirrings of lust. Climatically, the weather was on a par with that which Captain Scott, with true English aplomb, described as "somewhat inclement" in the last few sentences of his diary.

On the seventh day we went ashore, stayed long enough to find out that the price of beer was, like the landscape, out of this world, and returned with undue haste to the ship.

Within a week I was on both the beach and the unemployment register; I considered that the prospect of another voyage with Big Tam and his seagoing home for the chronically insane was less appealing than returning to the bosom of my family.

LIES, DAMNED LIES, AND RECRUITERS

When I got home I realised why I had left the bosom of my family so readily. The wife was in the kitchen preparing the mince for the children's dinner; the process was being somewhat delayed by the cow's reluctance to enter the mincer.

"Yir hame," she grunted, fishing in her cleavage for an errant curler. "Therr's some letters fur ye in the kitchen. Wan of them's fur a job interview."

My heart sank, for I had only written for one job, and that was at Sullom Voe. Sure enough, there was a letter from British Petroleum, inviting me to an interview at the Albany Hotel in Glasgow to assess my potential as an operator in their new oil terminal, which the letter stated was in an advanced stage of construction.

It struck me that if it was indeed in an advanced state of construction, somebody must have been going like the hammers of hell in the week since I had been there, but I was to discover in time that the corporate empire were past masters in the art of saying one thing and meaning quite another

After a few days I broached the subject with my wife, pointing out that, having just returned from Sullom Voe, I had little inclination to return.

The fair sex are long practised in using the bait of sexual allure to persuade their partners to accept their views. Sexual allure, however, was decidedly absent from my wife's inventory, and she favoured more direct methods. A well aimed kick in my impedimenta, followed by an asphyxiating armlock, persuaded me that perhaps the interview might be preferable to any further discussion on the matter.

The next week I left for the interview in Glasgow, having refused my wife's offer to kiss her goodbye for luck. There are some parts of a female anatomy which I am loth to kiss, and a buttock tattooed with the legend "Property of the United States Marine Corps" is one of them.

The interview was conducted by two English gentlemen (and there's a contradiction in terms for you) one of whom I never saw again. The other, John Seaman, who was later to become the first administration superintendent at Sullom Voe, did most of the talking. Much of the time

THE FIRST RULE OF RECRUITMENT - IF YOU CAN'T INSULT HIS INTELLIGENCE YOU'VE FOUND THE RIGHT MAN FOR THE JOB .

"...And the Council used some of the oil money we gave them to build this wall to keep the rain out..."

was spent going through the jobs I had done, my hobbies, what I did with my time when I was sober and the usual run of the mill questions.

"Have you ever stayed on an island?" asked Mr Seaman. Rather rashly, I pointed out that I had lived on one all my life, since Britain was an island. For some reason he was taken aback by this; I got the impression that he had not been privy to this information prior to the interview.

He then went on to give me a five minute pen picture of life in Shetland, a world of snow white beaches, waving sea grass, placid wee ponies contentedly chewing platefuls of cud, azure blue seas and snow white rollers curling gently in from the Atlantic.

"That's the picture," he concluded, sitting back and smiling expansively, "how does it sound to you?"

"Brilliant," said I, "but it sounds more like Tahiti than Shetland."

The two exchanged meaningful glances. "You've heard of it, then?" Mr Seaman's companion asked gloomily.

"I was there last week." I responded.

A doom -laden silence hung in the air like an cloud of elephant wind. Mr Seaman surreptitiously slipped a pile of heavily retouched recruitment brochures into his drawer, since he had no further use for them at this juncture.

"Of course," he went on, regaining his composure, "living in Shetland has its compensations." (I was to discover that the compensations in his case were to include flights home to the Surrey stockbroker belt every weekend.) "No crime, no pollution... ("yet"...muttered his companion under his breath) ...marvellous bird-watching and fishing, long summer nights and...ahem...easy access to the mainland. What do you think?"

What I thought was of little consequence. When one is married to a woman with the physique of a Sherman tank and a tendency to terminate discussion by ripping out one's arm and beating one about the head with the wet end, one learns that opinions are often best left unvoiced. I could think of a dozen sound reasons to say no, but the wish to stay alive was paramount, and I expressed my interest in the job offered, which was, at that stage, somewhat vague.

About three weeks later I received a letter stating that, subject to a medical, I would take up employment with BP in March 1978. The letter stated that I would undergo a period of training which would give me the necessary skills to operate all the hi-tech equipment being installed, that I would be expected to domicile in Shetland, and that a house would be provided for my family in a new estate.

The wife was over the moon. She didn't much like living in Rothesay and wanted a change of scene. I was tempted to suggest that in her case a few weeks on a hospitable planet like Mercury might fit the bill more appropriately, but thought better of it. My mother was also over the moon. "It's a staff job," said she. "They never sack staff people, only the workers." Mother had some rather fixed notions on job security which went out of the window in a big way during the Thatcher years. "Mind you," she said reflectively, "for God's sake stay out of the kitchens."

My problems of the past year were small beer compared to the crisis now facing me, and the only possible way out was to fail the medical. Unfortunately, despite years of self abuse, including eating my own cooking – under duress, of course – I was remarkably fit. I spent the two weeks prior to the medical swilling down Buckfast tonic wine and Old Spice and smoking so many cigarettes that I acquired a nicotine tan.

Unfortunately, my efforts were to no avail. I travelled to Glasgow for the medical, and ended in the doctor's waiting room with two others, one of whom was a nurse en route to Saudi, and the other a potential recruit, like myself, for Sullom Voe.

My fellow exile-to-be was certainly not cast in the corporate mould. Since he did not come from Glasgow, he was not called Jimmy, but he spoke a brand of English which led me to assume that he'd been educated somewhere in Upper Volta. This, as it turned out, was to his advantage, since he was so incomprehensible that nobody ever understood him well enough to contradict him.

He lumbered across the room, his huge knuckles leaving tracks on the axminster, and introduced himself as Jock Mackie. He was the first of my new workmates I was to meet, and I voiced a silent prayer that they wouldn't all be quite so neanderthal. He was quite convinced that he would pass his medical. "Ah've telt the doctor if a fail ah'll demand a post mortem," he snorted.

The only recollection I have of the medical is the doctor's chronic halitosis, which was like high grade mustard gas at ten paces. Despite my efforts I passed fit and went home to await the summons.

NEW HORIZONS

A letter crashed through the door like the crack of doom one dull February day, instructing me to report to Falkirk Technical College for a three-week induction course; the attendees were to be met by the training officer on the first night at a hotel, which would give us the opportunity to meet one another.

In the foyer of the hotel we encountered our first example of Corporate Man, whose hair was cut in regulation company fashion and held in place by liberal applications of Brylcreem. He had an electric smile which appeared to operated like Christmas tree lights, going on and off at the turn of a switch. The significance of the fact that he greeted everyone by name was lost on me at the time, but I have pondered on it since, for he had never met any of us before in his life.

There were fifteen of us, from all over the central belt of Scotland. Only one was a Shetland resident, an elderly character who bore a startling resemblance to Waldorf, the heckler in the Muppet Show.

The meal was our first introduction to the joys of living at someone else's expense, and as the night went on we soon developed an artificial rapport induced by a substantial intake of free drink.

My immediate neighbours at the table were a teuchter with a large beard, which partially concealed a tie the design of which was obviously based on parrot vomit, and on the other side a cadaverous character with a natty line in health service dentures.

The latter's decibel pitch rose in direct proportion to his alcohol intake, and when he discovered that we had both been in the navy at the same time, proclaimed loudly to the assembled company that this was indeed an amazing coincidence. Even more coincidentally, as well as Henry Tatler and myself, there were ninety-three thousand others in the navy at the time, and I had managed to go through the ensuing twenty years or so without meeting any of them.

I was beginning to get the distinct impression that my luck in this respect had changed decidedly for the worse.

Henry's glow quotient increased dramatically as the evening wore on, and eventually the training officer, Tom Slaven, remonstrated gently with him.

Displaying that amazing perception which was to make him a legend at Sullom Voe, he said: "You've been drinking, Henry!"

Henry eyed him blearily. "Of coursh I have," he enunciated slowly, "the drinksh ish free."

The teuchter, whose name was Angus McDonald, was a different animal entirely. He informed me that he had managed to serve a five-year apprenticeship and ten subsequent years as an electrician. The frightening aspect of his story was that he was chronically colour blind to the extent that he could only see in black and white.

He was moving to Shetland with his mistress and her six children, so obviously he was deficient in more than simply colour vision.

We soon started in earnest at Falkirk Technical College, learning the terminology of the oil industry, the types of valves and equipment, and the principles of crude oil and gases.

It occurred to me at a very early stage of my new career – I think it was about day three – that I wasn't making any sense out of it; in that respect the ensuing twelve years didn't change a thing.

Lectures were fun. One student, Fraser Andrew, always made a bee line for the front seat in class, and, within ten seconds of the lecturer breaking into full flood, had fallen fast asleep. This was most disconcerting for the student next to him, since he tended to rest his head on his neighbour's shoulder and snore loudly in sporadic bursts into his ear. Needless to say, it didn't do much for the lecturer's morale either.

At the conclusion of the course we all sat a test; I must have cheated, I suppose, because they didn't sack me.

Our next port of call was Dundee, where we were to learn the art of firefighting. This did little to inspire our confidence; the place wasn't even operational yet, and already they were planning fires.

The week started badly. None of us had any overalls; one could only conclude that staff in the Corporate Empire were expected to fight the odd conflagration in business suits. The training station, which was part of the local authority fire brigade, had some old overalls, and we were given these to wear.

"...and it comes out of the vaporiser, through the scrobifier and into the circumciser, where it is heated to a temperature of 275 degrees C...and that's when the mince starts burning..."

Two days after our arrival, a bigwig turned up from the Scottish Office to inspect the facility. Most of the personnel under training were real firemen, a highly disciplined and smart bunch indeed, and all the trainees were lined up on the training ground for inspection. Since we were dressed in overalls which would have been slung in the bin by any self-respecting Third World beggar, the powers that be decided to tuck us inconspicuously in the corner of the parade ground, in the hope that the bigwig might assume we were doing a group audition for Robinson Crusoe and had got lost on the way to the theatre.

Needless to say, our luck was out; the bigwig made his way with unerring aim in our direction, despite fervent prayers for divine intervention from the divisional officer. "Come to attention and at least try to look human," he snarled from the side of his mouth.

The politician looked at us with barely concealed distaste. "And what are you gentlemen doing here?" he enquired brightly.

"Freezing to bloody death!" came an exasperated mutter from the rear rank.

On the last day of the course we had an exercise with breathing apparatus which involved crawling around smoke-filled tunnels in the training centre. The teams were split into groups of seven and each man was given a number; the importance of each member of the team keeping in touch with the others was emphasised.

The first team went in and the rest of us waited outside. We could hear the sounds of shuffling as the team crawled through the tunnels, and heavy breathing amplified by the breathing sets. After a few minutes a voice squawked, "Number one, where are you?"

There was no response.

There was another bout of shuffling, and again the voice, slightly higher pitched this time, "Number one, where are you?"

Again there was no response.

After a few more minutes, the voice came again, this time like a lost soul in torment, "Number one... where are you?"

There was a gruff reply which solved the mystery: "Shut yir mooth, ye stupid bastard, you're number one."

We were sent home for some leave prior to the next stage of our training, two months on Occidental Oil's terminal on the island of Flotta in the Orkney Islands.

ORKNEY INTERLUDE

In Orkney we met up with the other group of recruits, most of whom were Shetlanders. We were based at two hotels in Kirkwall, and worked twelve -hour shifts on the terminal, which involved a round trip of around three quarters of an hour by car and boat.

Flotta was definitely not the fun spot of the Western Hemisphere. Parked in the middle of the former naval anchorage of Scapa Flow, it had been occupied during two world wars by large numbers of British servicemen, and an abundance of literature on the subject makes it clear that these veterans would have paid the enemy to invade and take it off their hands. The terminal itself was small in comparison with Sullom Voe, having one loading jetty and a couple of offshore loading points. We spent most of our time either making coffee or wandering behind people who knew what they were doing; Occidental Oil had more sense than to let us loose on our own, more so after one of our number managed to drown himself in oil during a tank transfer.

The security hut was situated at the jetty, since that was where all personnel landing at the terminal came ashore. During our stay, the guards rescued a baby seal from the Flow, and took it into their hut.

Since seals are a fairly rare form of wildlife to city dwellers – there hasn't been a seal sighting in Easterhouse since 1723 – the new arrival aroused some interest among our group. One nightshift we decided to pay the security hut a visit and see at first hand this denizen of the deep.

The waif was esconced in a cardboard box, swathed in blankets, and parked in front of a three-bar electric fire. Sharing the room, but not the bed, were two security guards. How they stood it was beyond me. It was hardly surprising that the seal was an orphan, for it suffered from body odour sufficient to make the eyes water; the room stank like a fish market after a six-month strike.

We spoke for some minutes to the guards, trying desperately to hold our breath. At length one of them looked at his watch and rose to his feet. "Come on, Pedro," he said to the seal, "time for your swim."

Pedro fixed him with the sort of reproachful expression which baby seals usually reserve for those large Canadian seal cullers who make a living out of beating baby seals over the head with baseball bats for the benefit of television wildlife programmes.

Despite his mute pleas, Pedro was dragged from his bed, carried down to the end of the jetty, and thrown into the sea.

Seals are aquatic animals, but even by seal standards Pedro could shift; he shot through the water like a torpedo, and was still doing a frantic American crawl when he was halfway up the beach. One got the clear impression that the therapy of being hauled from a mega-tropical environment and hurled into the sub zero waters of Scapa Flow was not his notion of therapy.

Our group was billeted in the Regal Hotel, which belied its lofty title. The residents' lounge had the level of natural light which one would expect in a Dickensian workhouse, primarily because at some time in the distant past, probably around the sixteeenth century, the window cleaner had gone on strike in protest over Orkney's free transfer from Norway to Scotland, and daylight was blocked by the accumulation of aeons of accumulated grime. The cuisine was also workhouse quality, and not even Oliver Twist would have been desperate enough to ask for more.

I shared a room with a chap called Sandy Grant, who was a cleanliness freak and spent most of his waking moments in the bath. He had a fetish about washing clothes, and the basin in the hotel room was permanently filled with socks and Y-fronts. I once made the mistake of leaving a brand new sweater on my bed, and returned to the room to find it washed and hanging out to dry. It was certainly clean, but I never wore it again; the torso had shrunk to about three inches long and the arms stretched to about three fathoms.

It was at Flotta that the redoubtable Henry Tatler discovered the benefits of the cheque book for the first time. Using his new found system of financial management, Henry became hopelessly infatuated with Highland Park Whisky, a particularly deadly product of Orkney. As a result, much of Henry's time off shift was spent furthering this relationship, which reduced him the state of mental ineptitude which one would normally only expect to find in a cabinet minister.

One evening Henry had retired, having overdosed early. Within five minutes of his disappearance his wife telephoned; needless to say, Henry

"... As he was saying, it's amazing how the piquant bouquet of a bottle of Chardonnay '74 complements eleven pints of export..."

was by that time well into orbit and could not be roused.

The rest of us were engrossed in viewing a hysterical comedy show featuring the efforts of an alleged team of Scottish footballers which had gone to Argentina to bring back the World Cup. The show was at its funniest when the phone rang again, and all through the remainder of the evening our entertainment was punctuated by constant telephone calls from Mrs Tatler trying to contact her husband.

By one in the morning we had had enough, and went to reception for the pass key for Henry's room.

The deceased was not a pretty sight; he bore a remarkable resemblance to one of those ancient Pictish chieftains – the ones that have been dead for about two thousand years and been mummified in peat bogs. He was sprawled out on his bed with his teeth out and his mouth open, clad only in his Y-fronts. The whisky fumes in the room were enough to knock out a bull moose.

Henry couldn't be roused, and appeared to be dead; there was a vain request for a volunteer to give him mouth to mouth. We eventually applied more effective resuscitation by throwing a bucket of water over him and informed him that his wife was trying to contact him.

At two o'clock in the morning in the residents lounge, the post match autopsy was still in full flood. It had been suggested that the Scottish manager would only bring the World Cup back to Scotland if his team threw away their boots and took Armalites on to the pitch; at this point the door opened and Henry stalked in, dressed to the nines in his catalogue safari suit, and reeking of Brut, to ask, "Any of you guys fancy going out for a pint?"

Henry claimed that we had been specially selected from three hundred applicants for the job; they had probably used the same criteria to pick mice and hamsters for research laboratories.

There was certainly nothing standard about our group; at least two had undergone psychiatric treatment, one was a kleptomaniac, most were sex maniacs, and one had read *No Mean City* so many times that he thought he was the hero of the book.

Frank Cornell, who was the kleptomaniac, was a master of his art; he was a plausible rogue, with a magnetic personality and fingers to match. He subscribed to a variation on the Marxist tenet to the effect that property (owned by others) is theft, and operated a one-man wealth redistribution campaign to redress the balance in his favour via wholesale larceny. His prizes ranged from sheepskin rugs to jewellery; he was once overheard telephoning his wife with some bad news: "I can't get you that gold chain for your birthday, dear: they've got them all locked up!"

One day Frank appeared at the hotel with a new digital watch. In the late seventies digital watches were still a novelty, and were relatively expensive. Sure enough, his acquisition was spotted by Henry, who was still suffering from cheque book fever.

Henry established the name of the shop from which Frank had obtained his hi-tech marvel, and made his way there at speed, since his informant had told him that the stock of digital watches was limited.

He entered the premises, and after some searching, found a watch identical to that worn by Frank. He took his purchase to the counter and produced his cheque-book with a practised flourish, based on Kirk Douglas' quick draw style as demonstrated in *The Gunfight at the OK Corral*.

This display of dexterity so impressed the jeweller that he engaged Henry in conversation, and the dialogue got round to Henry's purchase.

"Marvellous watches, these," Henry waxed lyrically. "Never lose a second. Ma mate told me aboot them; in fact he bought one in here yesterday."

It crossed Henry's mind that he had said something wrong, but he couldn't think what. The jeweller's visage grew a shade of vivid purple and his right eye twitched uncontrollably; he advanced rapidly around the counter towards Henry, growling ominously:

"I'd like a word with this mate of yours; nobody bought a digital watch in here yesterday, but some bastard stole one."

There was a ten-second freeze-frame as God hit the pause button on the world. When the world restarted, Henry, his cheque-book, and his digital watch had a good head start.

The Regal had two bars, a lounge bar and a public bar, the only significant difference in decor being that the former had a second-hand carpet acquired from a long-defunct cinema, and was staffed by a New Zealand barmaid who rolled her eye seductively at her customers. This ploy was less effective than she might have hoped, since she kept the other eye in reserve, along with her teeth, in the jar of pickled eggs which was the establishment's sole foray into what is nowadays described as Pub Grub.

The public bar was rather less pretentious; the carpet was renewed weekly with the sweepings from the nearby carpenter's shop, and the clientele was provided by the sweepings of Orcadian society. One evening I was imbibing in this intimate ambience with Sandy Grant, when a group of inebriates entered and sat down at the next table. Apart from being drunk, the only thing they had in common was their colour – they looked like extras from the ethnic minority part of the Black and White Minstrel Show.

It transpired that they were asphalters doing a job on the post office roof. It further transpired that they had got drunk on the proceeds of their latest delivery of the bitumastic paint for the job, which they had sold as soon as it arrived. They had stopped using it because it was more profitable to sell it and use black gloss as a substitute, and also because most of the specialist paint had ended up on their hands and faces, and they couldn't get it off.

They were flying at thirty thousand feet when they entered the bar, and a few huge rounds of drink soon elevated them to the rarefied upper atmosphere. It turned out that they were resident in the Regal, but used the public bar because they were barred from the lounge. They were having a farewell party for their chargehand, who was departing for the mainland the next day.

We encountered them again the following morning, at what passed for breakfast; their entrée for this repast was a bottle of Famous Grouse, which was fatally injured by the time the meal started. As a consequence of this one of the party collapsed and almost made the Guinness Book of Records by drowning in his cornflakes.

His companions managed to remain reasonably vertical throughout the meal, although their condition progressively deteriorated. When the waiter came through from the kitchen with the fire hose to clear their table, the chargehand lurched over to us with a battered cigarette dangling from his mouth.

"Huv any of yiz goat a light?" he asked, burping solicitously.

Sandy gave him a light, managing to singe his eyebrows before making contact with the end of his cigarette.

"Did you enjoy your breakfast?" Sandy asked.

The chargehand stared vacantly at him. "Ah cannae remember," said he, turning to his fellow gourmets. "Can ony of youse remember whether ah enjoyed ma breakfast?"

The celebrants decided to accompany their departing friend to Kirkwall airport. On his arrival, the airport staff were loth to allow him onto the plane, and called the constabulary to persuade the traveller that it might perhaps be advisable for him to keep his body on the ground until it had been rejoined by his brain. His friends, however, successfully prevailed upon the forces of law and order to let him board the aircraft.

After takeoff he had a new lease of life, and was refuelled, courtesy of British Airways, with a large quantity of miniature whiskies.

On arrival at Glasgow he went to retrieve his luggage and collapsed on the carousel, doing four circuits before they could get him off.

THE GOURMET

Jock Mackie was on the verge of marriage, and this new enterprise made heavy demands on his budget. He ate as if there was no tomorrow, and habitually turned up for meals wearing a long black overcoat with huge pockets. He used the overcoat to ensure that not only was the table cleared of food but of cutlery and china as well, the latter being relocated in his bottom drawer in readiness for the impending nuptials.

There was little doubt that the culinary standards of the Regal left a lot to be desired; rumour had it that the chef was on the run from a biological warfare establishment. Steak appeared regularly on the menu but seldom on the tables; it always seemed to be off just before we came in for our meal and was substituted by corned beef hash or some similar delicacy.

One day, however, there was steak on both the menu and the table. Significantly the hotel had as its guest the then Secretary of State for Scotland, who was making a whistle-stop nationwide tour in a vain bid to convince the country that the government knew what it was doing.

The honourable gentleman had the misfortune to pick the table between the asphalters and big Jock, who started off by demanding a fish entrée; he hated fish, but he needed some fish knives to make up his set.

When Jock saw the Secretary's steak arrive, his eyes lit up, and he ordered one for himself in his own inimitable style, grabbing the waiter by the throat and intoning slowly: "Mind and gie me a decent sized bit noo, an' bring the horns wi' it, ah waant tae be sure ah'm eatin' the real thing."

The waiter gave Jock his steak and beat a hasty retreat. Jock assailed the meat in vain with his knife, hacking away ineffectually without making any impact. His face grew red with exertion and frustration. "Waiter!"

he bellowed, the megadecibel roar sweeping across the dining room like the shock wave from Krakatoa.

The waiter, however, was blessed with more sense than courage, and had barricaded himself in the kitchen.

Jock was strong on initiative; realising that his seated posture was inhibiting the amount of purchase he was getting with his knife, he stood on to his chair and renewed his attack on the steak.

This display of resourcefulness was lost on the Secretary of State; one of the asphalters had just offered him a swig of Lanliq and he made a hasty exit from the dining room.

Two days later Tom Slaven turned up unannounced, having been summoned by the hotel manager, who had taken a very dim view of Jock's eating habits.

There was a heart to heart between Jock and Corporate Man, which concluded with Jock being disciplined by being sent home on full pay, until such time as he should be called upon to go to Shetland.

This draconian and unjust punishment was not lost on the rest of us. At lunch the next day, we all ate standing on our chairs.

THE GENTLE SEX

Occidental Oil had block bookings with British Airways, which enabled us to fly home for weekends. It also gave us the facility to bring up our nearest and dearest, and even our wives.

One who took advantage of the opportunity to bring up his wife was Joe Bryant. Joe was a small man, who resembled Andy Capp without the cap, but laboured under the delusion that he looked like Paul Newman.

He had successfully booked his wife on the plane, and we were all well warned in advance of her impending arrival; we had to be on our best behaviour, since she was "awfy religious".

Joe's wife duly arrived, and went out with a bunch of the lads that evening for a few drinks.

It did occur to us as the evening progressed that for someone with religious convictions she had a prodigious appetite for bevvy. It was suggested during a council of war in the gents' powder room the Good Lord would have to turn the North Sea into Smirnoff to keep her going.

We had been warned by wee Joe, however, that we should maintain the standards of behaviour appropriate in the company of a lady, and this we did until well into the evening, when, it appeared to wee Joe's wife, he had omitted to get a round in.

"Get yir haun' in yer pocket, ye miserable wee bastard," quoth his paragon of virtue, "mine's a double voddy!"

After this exchange of gay repartee the night loosened up somewhat.

The hotel telephone was a kiosk situated in the hallway and there was always a queue for its use in the evening. Its soundproofing was negligible, and it was difficult to avoid hearing one side of telephone conversations.

"If that's Henry on the phone for me tell him I'll call him back after Coronation Street..."

One night a substantial queue had formed, and Henry Tatler had gone into the kiosk.

He spoke to his wife for a minute or so, asking the stock questions about the kids and the weather. Then came the punchline:

"That's all I've got to say, love, put Scamp on..."

The queue suddenly woke from their torpor and exchanged wide-eyed glances, silently asking each other the question:

"Scamp? Scamp? Who the hell is Scamp?"

Henry wasn't slow in putting us out of our misery.

"Who's a good dog?" he crooned into the mouthpiece; he didn't wait for an answer, but continued, "Is Scamp missing his daddy? Woof! woof!"

The conversation with Scamp was punctuated with proclamations of everlasting love and intimate endearments, and lasted three times longer than Henry's conversation with his wife.

He was ever after known as "Woof" Tatler.

After two months we left Flotta – in my case at least, none the wiser than when I had arrived – and were sent home on pay to await events.

I was home a few days when I received a telegram from my former employers on the paddlesteamer, asking me to get in touch. I telephoned them, to be asked if, since I was on leave, I'd be willing to sail as relief chief steward for a few weeks.

About six weeks later the ship was berthed in Ayr. I was taking some bags of rubbish ashore – the chief steward's job description was a very elastic one – when wee Joe turned up at the gangplank.

"Whit are you daein' here?" he asked incredulously.

I told him I was passing the time waiting for word from BP; it transpired that he'd been in Shetland for a month.

Thank God, thought I, they've forgotten all about me!

They hadn't.

GOOD MORNING, CAMPERS...

On August 18th 1978, I landed at Sumburgh Airport, Shetland. It was a fine summer day, the sort of weather which brings the ethereal beauty of the islands home to the visitor. I caught a taxi to Lerwick, about twenty miles north, my letter of instruction having directed me to go to Staneyhill Camp.

That in itself puzzled me; horror stories were beginning to filter into the tabloid press about the terminal's construction camps, and we had been categorically assured that we would be accommodated in a hotel. It was already beginning to dawn on us that categoric assurances from the Corporate Hierarchy were a little like the Ten Commandments, somewhat open to interpretation.

Categoric assurances apart, Staneyhill camp was just that, a camp. It had formerly been occupied by construction workers, and still bore the scars of its ordeal. There was a block which contained the kitchen, the cafeteria and the recreation facilities, which consisted of a television, most of a dartboard, and a three-legged pool table with more bald patches than Paul Daniels.

The accommodation was in three blocks, each of which consisted of a long corridor with rooms along each side. It looked like a collection of portacabins, which was, in fact, precisely what it was.

The manager, who also did most of the cooking, bore a remarkable resemblance to one of the Morlocks from H.G. Wells' *Time Machine*: the little guys who lived underground and only came up top for a feed of humans living on the surface. He had a forehead about an inch deep, sunken eyes and a permanently sagging lower lip. My first thought on meeting him was that he must be the role model for the typical *Sun* reader.

He showed me to my room, pointing out the rules en route. For instance, no laughing out loud, but occasional smiles were permissible by prior arrangement with the management. Fortunately, there was no legislation to cover rending of garments or gnashing of teeth, which I considered the only display of emotion likely to affect the residents of Staneyhill.

Each resident or, more appropriately, inmate, had a room of his own. I was puzzled to note that on both of the inside walls the plasterboard was patched. Apparently the previous residents had lived two to a room and tended to drink a lot. It appears that when one of the residents ran out of tins of life support, he would shout the password: "Pass us a can, somebody!" His beneficiary might be three rooms away and, rather than take a drink to him, would simply punch a hole in the wall and pass it to his neighbour, who would pass it to his room-mate who would repeat the process until six people and sheets of plasterboard later, the beer had arrived at its destination.

By the time I had settled in the inmates had returned from work and it was time for dinner. The camp was well-filled with both operators and firemen, although the latter were to move fairly soon to accommodation ships near the terminal.

I spoke to a few of those whom I had met before, and the same thread ran through all the conversations: paraphrased roughly, it went something like:

"Sod this for a game of soldiers I'm not sticking this I'll be out in a month I'm not bringing the wife and kids up here there's nothing to do wait till you taste the cooking did you bring any blue videos up with you..."

It seemed mutterings of discontent were prevalent.

ENTER THE MUFF

The first day had been relatively full, and I decided to turn in early. In the small hours, around three in the morning, I was awakened by an ear splitting racket in the corridor, rather like a cat having its goolagongs removed without benefit of anaesthetic. Staggering along the corridor was an apparition in a state of terminal inebriation, who, judging by the shrieks of agony, appeared to be sodomising a mouth organ.

This, it turned out, was the legendary Charlie "Muff" Yeats, whose nickname had nothing to do with hand warmers, but was more sexually orientated.

By comparison with Muff, Walter Mitty had no imagination whatsoever; Muff's life story was an extended fantasy spanning at least ten years more than he had spent on the planet. He had been a professional footballer, and had known Brian Clough well enough to have a conversation with him.

The conversation consisted of two words from Brian Clough: "You're sacked!"

Muff had then joined the Navy or the Black Watch or the Jehovah's Witnesses, dependent upon how much he'd had to drink or to whom the story was being told.

He played the pipes in the Black Watch band at a Scotland-England international at Wembley; this was quite an achievement for a man lacking two fingers on his chanter hand.

During the course of the match, Muff was in the Royal Box with the rest of the band when he felt a tap on his shoulder.

He turned round, and there was the Duchess of Kent, who asked:

"Charlie, gonny go and get me a pie and a bovril?"

After half-time Muff went to the toilet to relieve himself, and there met an elderly gent in a grey gaberdine who offered him a swig from his half bottle.

Muff accepted the drink. "Wi' the kind of money yir wife's oan ye should be able tae afford better whisky than this," he told the Duke of Edinburgh.

EARLY DAYS

The following day I went to work with the rest of the inmates. The twenty-five miles or so from Lerwick to Sullom Voe were hardly scenically inspiring. Miles and miles of peat bog and woebegone sheep. As we neared the terminal the impact of six thousand or so construction workers made itself felt. We didn't see a lot of them on the road, but most of the

Chatting up the local talent was a risky business indeed...

sheep seemed to be wearing lipstick.

Sullom Voe was not a pretty sight; a bit like the Somme on early closing day, only muddier. Our group was based in a portacabin designated the Temporary Control Cabin, or TCC.

This edifice, the cornerstone of terminal oil movements operations, was to be our base for months to come. It formed a U shape, consisting of a control room, a supervisor's office, and a messroom.

At least there was plenty to eat; every other building on the site seemed to be a canteen, and we spent the first couple of months jumping from one to the other, stuffing ourselves with rolls and scotch pies.

Apart from eating, there was little else to do. All kinds of grandiose plant familiarisation programmes were conceived, and just as quickly shelved; there was a distinct lack of enthusiasm for terminal walkabouts in two feet of mud.

One attempt at education failed when our supervisor took us to the effluent treatment plant in the hope of furthering our knowledge of its intricacies. We were parked at the edge of a large hole in the ground looking at a maze of pipework while our mentor attempted to explain where everything was coming from, where it was going, and what would happen to it before it got there. This masterly lecture lasted until his glasses steamed up and he came to a grinding halt. "That's funny," he muttered, "This bit's not on the drawing!"

"Not surprising," said a wit at the back of the group. "That's a drawing of the canteen plumbing system!"

About this time we were allocated shifts, although it was to be a few weeks before shift work would commence. There were to be five shifts, and I was allocated B Shift. New starts were still arriving in droves, and one of them was to be our new shift foreman.

His name was Norman Walton. He was short, fat, splay footed and had about three teeth; in fact, he bore a startling resemblance to a pregnant womble. Despite these apparent shortages in the good looks department, he seemed to have a magnetic attraction to the opposite sex, and pulled the birds in the most amazing fashion. This was surprising in view of his one real minus point; he had by far the worst case of athlete's foot I have ever seen in my life. If his feet had been dogs they would have been shot out of hand.

He was English, and his last job had been at Flixborough, a chemical plant which had self destructed rather abruptly a few years before; the fact that he was allegedly watching a football match fifty miles away when the explosion took place did not absolve him from blame in the eyes of the shift, who considered him to be a bit of a haemorrhoid.

The shift supervisor was Chick Faulds, who was a very bitter man, believing that with his track record he should have been terminal manager. He had previously been manager of a refinery in Canada which had closed before it opened. Rumour had it that his superiors decided to cut their losses and shut down rather than having Chick shut it down in a rather more dramatic fashion. He spent all his time at work engaged in forward planning, all of it relating to a croft he was building; I came rapidly to the conclusion that he was nearly as interested in Sullom Voe as I was. The upper echelons of management were a race apart, primarily because they were almost exclusively Welsh. I had met the odd Welshman before, and I was to discover at Sullom Voe that odd Welshmen were the norm.

They suffer collective national delusions, like the belief that they are all marvellous bass baritones and, even more bizarrely, that they have a national team which can play rugby. They all sounded like Neil Kinnock, and were, for the most part, almost as convincing.

MUTTERINGS OF DISCONTENT

By the autumn of 1978, pressure grew among the immigrant community, or Soothmoothers as the Shetlanders affectionately called us, for the company to provide the promised housing. The housing officer was a pleasant chap called Alastair Bellamy, who was well qualified in the science of housing management, since he was a ship's radio officer.

His lot ashore was not a happy one. The housing allocation system was supposedly based on company service first and family need second, but in reality it was incomprehensible and defied logic; one lad was housed almost immediately on his arrival, simply because the company mixed him up with his father, who had more company service than Methuselah had years, while the son had been with the Corporate Empire about five minutes. It was rumoured that the hapless housing officer took more bribes than a Nigerian customs official, but if he was taking a few bob on the side, he needed it to keep him going in Valium, for he was a walking ulcer.

Just before we were due to go on shift, the company allocated us to operational areas. This caused considerable discontent, since many of us were to be sent to areas which were not of our choosing. I was allocated to the jetties. One was just about to become operational, and berthing trials were to commence shortly.

A meeting was arranged between the operations manager and the malcontents, and the Corporate Entity explained the logic behind the company's decision to us. He had a habit of prefacing every sentence with "To be perfectly frank and blunt," and we soon came to realise that what would follow would be anything but, since empty Welsh rhetoric was his forte.

The logic in my case, he said, was self evident, since I had been to sea. I was at pains to point out that my seagoing career had consisted of frying eggs, which was not exactly appropriate experience for berthing three hundred thousand ton tankers. He looked straight in my eyes and told me probably the most repeated falsehood in the Corporate Book of Terminological Inexactitudes: "Don't worry," said he, "There will be somebody there who knows what they're doing."

The debate became somewhat heated as the "Stuff you pal, I can get a better job in Saudi" mentality began to surface.

At that point the door opened, and a messenger from On High entered. "I bear ye glad tidings," quoth he. "Verily ye have all been given houses!"

There was a stunned silence; one cretin leapt to his feet and did an impromptu jig, which brought the proceedings to an abrupt and unsatisfactory conclusion.

We went on leave a week or so later, and on our return discovered that Frank Cornell had gone off on the sick, presumably at the shock of being prematurely housed. He never came back; the company kept him on the books for a year on full pay until eventually, the galley wireless had it, he was visited at home in Culture City by Mr Seaman.

Frank had taken the elementary precaution of claiming his allowances for moving up, which ran to quite a few bob, and Mr Seaman suggested that he should either get back to work and move his family to Shetland, or resign and pay the money back. Pete pointed out that he was in the throes of a severe nervous breakdown which made him prone to outbreaks of murderous violence; any suggestion that he owed the company money could well trigger such an outbreak, with the Corporate Servant as the recipient. The Corporate Servant felt that, in the circumstances, the company could afford to write off their loss, and lent Frank his Parker pen to sign the resignation letter. He left with the letter, but without the pen.

Just before we were due to go on nightshift, the company were prevailed upon to express their appreciation to their long suffering staff by providing the appropriate victuals, both nutritional and alcoholic, for a party at Staneyhill. Large quantities of glow lotion were provided by the company, and were consumed with gusto by the celebrants; as a result of this over indulgence the meal was consumed in an alcoholic stupor, which, given the fact that the manager had excelled himself and produced a meal which was digestible, was rather a shame. Following the repast, the congregation moved to the recreation room and assailed the liquid refreshments with enthusiasm.

The festivities were in full flood when a dispute arose between Jock Mackie and a member of the camp staff over some drink which had allegedly gone missing.

Up to this point the staff member's wife had been promenading around the room, vainly trying to look feminine and seductive in what looked rather like a large multi-coloured quilt cover; in reality she looked rather like Cyril Smith impersonating Imelda Marcos.

Although the altercation between Jock and her husband had been halted by some timely diplomatic intervention, she obviously felt that her husband's honour had been impugned, and decided to exact retribution by throwing a chair at Jock.

Since she had the physique of an overweight Sumo wrestler, the chair hurtled across the room with the velocity of a Scud missile; unfortunately it had the accuracy to match, and struck the wall about an inch from my left ear, one of the chair legs impaling itself in the wall. This did not have the desired effect, since her intended victim was about three seats away from me; it did, however, rouse Big Jock into a murderous frenzy, and he made for her husband at a considerable rate of knots, spitting teeth and fury and promising instant dismemberment.

Four of us managed to get hold of him before he got to his intended victim, who was advancing bravely in the Italian fashion and was going full astern for the nearest exit. Trying to hold Jock back was, however, rather like stopping a Tiger tank with a snowball; although his victim made good his escape, Jock scattered the rest of us like chaff in a typhoon, and in seconds the party venue looked like a casualty clearing station.

LEARNING THE ROPES

Shift work made little difference to our lifestyle; days were spent wandering aimlessly about the site, and the silent hours in endless games of Monopoly. Training logs were optimistically issued, in the full knowledge that nobody in their right mind would venture out in the hours of darkness, for the site was a quagmire.

Buckie Bob Brown, however, was cast in a more heroic mould, and decided that two o'clock in the morning was as good a time as any to familiarise himself with the effluent plant. Bob was a large, slow-moving character, who spoke with such deliberation that it took him a day and a half to finish a sentence. His departure from the TCC into the great unknown was regarded with some disfavour by his comrades, since he had picked his moment wisely, having just lifted the pot after a heavy game of brag.

Wandering around the effluent plant in daylight was fraught with hazard; at night it was sheer death wish material. Bob in his wisdom had heightened the risk by deciding to walk backwards, and within minutes had fallen into a large water-filled crater. His squawks for assistance over the radio wakened the fire department from their slumbers, and a rescue squad arrived to find Bob groping around in the darkness looking for his glasses, which had fallen off during his escapade.

In the course of rescuing Bob's glasses, one of the fireman also fell into the hole, and spent five minutes swimming around in an attempt to locate the missing glasses before Bob rather shamefacedly interrupted his efforts ...

"...Ahem...you're looking in the wrong hole...it's that one over there..."

It is widely believed that the spirit of mutual detestation which characterises relations between the two departments to this day stems back to that night in 1978.

Oil was threatening to come ashore, and it was decided that it might be not a bad idea to tell us what was about to happen. We were accordingly told to muster in the administration building, where we would be given a résumé of the plans. This made a pleasant change; information was usually so scanty that we were phoning *The Shetland Times* to find out what was happening at work.

It should be understood that we had very few dealings with management; as far as we were concerned they were people who came to work in suits, which exempted them from going out in the rain, and should have been back home in Wales where they belonged.

We looked forward to the presentation with some trepidation; after all, it was to be our first encounter with a member of the Corporate Hierarchy which held our futures in its thrall.

The oil movements superintendent, Jack York, was a different animal. He wore a suit, certainly, but there his pretensions came to a stop. He had two teeth randomly scattered across his gums, and spoke with a decidedly non-corporate Geordie accent.

His first experience of oil had been during National Service in the King's Navy in the late 1940s, when he had become involved in the early days of helicopters. Since there was a fuel crisis at the time, the helicopters did little flying, which was just as well, as they were remarkably unpredictable and tended to drop out of the sky with alarming frequency.

Able Seaman York soon hit upon a way to resolve the problem, and augmented his meagre service pay by selling helicopter fuel to the owners of Austin Sevens. As a result of his entrepreneurial spirit, the helicopters stayed safely grounded, and the peace of the countryside was rent by the thunder of exploding Austin Sevens.

Jack left the Navy and joined the Company, which posted him to the Middle East, where he soon struck up a relationship with the locals, and used his new authority to promote them to positions of responsibility.

The former teaboy, who showed an aptitude for chemistry, was made Plant Analytical Chemist. No expense was spared in providing him with equipment to carry out his job, and his benefactor paid for the tin mug which constituted the inventory of his laboratory. His task was to analyse the various liquids produced by the plant. He would draw off a mugful, taste it, and pronounce his verdict on the contents, e.g. oil, fresh water, salt water or sewage.

Jack's presentation reflected his years of experience... "Right, lads...smoke if ye want to...ah bliddy am...now this bliddy first oil ashore business...if yer goin' for a piss son, can ye get me a coffee...black no sugar...Christ what a bliddy head ah've got...as ah was sayin' lads...thanks, son...Christ...it's got bliddy sugar in it...!"

His audience listened enraptured; after the meeting there was a heated discussion about his presentation.

"I counted a hundred and fifty seven bliddys and fourteen Jesus Christs!" said Angus MacDonald, who aspired to the post of shift mathematician.

"No, there were more than that," said another, "I was watching you ticking them off, and you missed three when you were sharpening your pencil..."

Events were to prove that most of us had been too busy counting the curses to notice the bits in between.

Staneyhill was beginning to fill with a large influx trapped by the company's recruitment dragnet; all of the new arrivals had been taken into the fold on the basis of having some expertise in the oil or gas industry.

Some had been transferred from other BP sites on the UK mainland; it soon became obvious that many of the latter were not bringing their expertise to Sullom Voe, but were transferring their incompetence from elsewhere, having been furnished, for the worst possible reasons, with glowing references from their previous managers.

Libya produced a large number of new recruits; King Idris had been deposed by Ghadaffi, who is not nearly as crazy as the *Sun* would have us believe; he was shrewd enough to deport his British unwanted direct to Sullom Voe, and they certainly struck terror into our hearts.

DAMAGEMENT

The upper echelons, supervisors, managers and the like, were based in hotels in Lerwick, so at least we only had to be civil to them during working hours. It became apparent pretty quickly that the problems the company was having in finding staff were not confined to the lower classes, since some of the supervisory staff obviously did not have both oars in the water.

I walked into the messroom one morning at shift change, to find the supervisor of the offgoing shift passing the time awaiting his relief by playing darts on the back of the messroom door. This in itself was reprehensible enough, since darts is a pursuit of the obese and the working classes; the fact that he was using a nine-inch Bowie knife as a dart made it all the more strange. This supervisor, whose name was Bert McFarlane, was nicknamed Alaska Bert, although there was a perception afoot that the nearest he had been to Alaska was the baked variety.

He had all the trappings of what we now call yuppiedom; he owned a Porsche and a Rolex and wore tinted glasses, presumably to dim the glare from the fearsome pattern of his suit material. He kept a teddy bear on his office desk, and was rumoured to have long philosophical discussions with it (he called it "him" but we couldn't find any evidence to support this) during the night-shifts. It was further rumoured that the teddy bear was his technical adviser, which might account for his somewhat eccentric methods of plant management.

He had an aim in life which he pursued with manic zeal; he spent all his free time in Shetland trying to cure virginity in the female population. This, the cynic might consider, would require no great effort, for the incidence of virginity nowadays is hardly of epidemic proportions, but Bert also provided a comprehensive after sales service. He could be seen most nights in dark corners of the seedier hostelries of Lerwick, waving his Rolex-encased wrist and shouting, "Want a lift in my Porsche?" at anything remotely resembling the opposite sex.

As a consequence of his divine crusade, Bert took an early bath when the company began hinting he should move up. He was astute enough to realise that when he brought his wife up from the mainland she might find out just why he wasn't exactly superstud when he came home on leave.

OIL

In October 1978 first oil came ashore and was hailed as a major achievement. We all received a little plastic cube with a globule of oil in it, much as a couple of centuries before the white man had impressed his good intentions on the Red Indian by giving him strings of beads.

The celebrations, however, were somewhat marred when someone pointed out that, though the oil had come ashore, it wasn't all where it should be. There had been some discrepancy between the amount of oil pumped ashore and the amount in the tanks, and the accountants were scratching their heads and other parts of their anatomy, trying to figure out where the missing oil had gone. When a few days later the ice melted on the Houb, a large loch in the middle of the terminal which would be used as a final holding basin for ballast water, the mystery was solved, for the surface was covered with oil.

First Oil Ashore had become First Oil Slick; suggestions that another plastic cube was in order were given short shrift.

Mini skimmers were put on the Houb in an attempt to clean up the mess, and portable pumps were sited onshore. The pumps were a major headache, for they were always stopping for no apparent reason, and required considerable swinging on a starting handle to restore them to life. During the course of a particularly unpleasant nightshift an operator reached the end of his tether with a recalcitrant pump and heaved the starting handle into the Houb. His colleagues were not slow to follow this sterling example of dedication to the job, and within a week there wasn't a starting handle to be had on site; not above sea level, anyway.

Tanker trials commenced with the arrival, and successful berthing and loading, of the Shell tanker *Donovania*. This was the cue for the souvenir hunters to pour down to the jetties in droves and fill bottles of the first crude oil to be exported from Sullom Voe.

Naturally I took a couple for myself; we had no Wally Dugs on the fireplace, and I thought a couple of coke bottles filled with oil would enhance the decor of the front room. I successfully transported the bottles to Staneyhill and put them on top of the wardrobe out of harm's way.

They both blew during the night; I had a great deal of difficulty convincing the manager that I must have brought the oil in on my boots, since he wanted to know how it had gone not only all over the bed, but eight feet up the wall as well.

The jetties were manned by Shetlanders, mostly ex-seamen or fishermen. It seemed, however, that the recruitment problems which had plagued the company were not entirely confined to mainland recruits, since at least one jetty operator on my shift had obviously gone to the January sales for his quota of grey matter. On his second night at work he complained bitterly to the supervisor that someone had stolen his sleeping bag from the top of his locker; it did not occur to him that the supervisor might be less concerned at the alleged theft than the reason that he had brought a sleeping bag to work in the first place. One of his recreations was "flashing" at tankers as they came in to berth. This was indeed a practice requiring great courage, since most of the time even brass monkeys would have been at risk.

During my spell on the jetties I took up painting sailing ships on dinner plates to pass the time. This was an engrossing pastime, and much more interesting than tying up tankers, but difficulties arose when it came to putting a border round the plates, since it meant drawing a perfect circle around the inner side of the rim.

I eventually had a brain-wave, and bought a can of aerosol spray paint from a garage. I took my purchase back to Staneyhill to test my theory out. The plan I had conceived was to put a dessert plate in the centre of the dinner plate, masking off the painting and leaving a perfect circle which would allow me to spray the outer edge.

It worked a treat; there was a perfect blue circle on the plate as I had planned. Unfortunately there was also one on the beige carpet where the plate had been.

In all honesty, it considerably enhanced the appearance of the room; I regard tidiness as a disease on a par with those one reads about on toilet walls. I moved to three different rooms during my stay in Staneyhill, and after each move the management bricked up my old residence.

In the early days Staneyhill had three cars; two were used to get people to work and one was left behind for leisure purposes. Money seemed to be no object; Sullom Voe must have been taking the annual production of the Triumph factory's Dolomites, for there were more Dolomites on Shetland than there were rabbits. This was just as well, for the attrition rate was frightening – the roadsides of the terminal were strewn with dead and dying Dolomites.

The fatalities had little to do with the craftsmanship of the British worker, and the total lack of maintenance was only partly responsible. Some cars went through a whole lifetime – albeit short – without ever experiencing that ecstatic surge of power which comes from moving up from first to second gear, while others were the subject of shift sweeps, based on how long the engine would run at full revs with the oil warning light on.

Soon, however, the company decided that buses would be a less expensive method of getting us to work, and set up a shift bus service, using a local company as contractors.

The service got off to a very shaky start indeed; the bus was scheduled to leave Lerwick at 0700 and arrive at Sullom Voe an hour later. During the course of the first week one driver, not over-endowed with grey matter, managed to arrive at Sullom Voe at the time he was scheduled to leave Lerwick; since he was by nature a solitary person, the fact that he had a fifty seater bus to himself apparently troubled him not at all. This went down like a lead balloon with the shift which was awaiting relief, and the supervisor was restrained with difficulty from ramming a wheel spanner into a delicate portion of his sedentary area, it being pointed out to him that the driver might have difficulty getting the bus back to Lerwick if he had to stand all the way.

A regular driver was soon put on the run; his sole virtue was that he turned up on time and usually remembered to bring his bus. He drove one-handed, since he needed the other one for his glass of whisky, which was subject to constant replenishment from the bottle under his seat. Since his substantial intake gave him a personal glow, he was warm enough to dispense with the bus heater.

His passengers, however, were not so fortunate, for the temperature inside the bus was sub-zero, and was further reduced by the driver's insistence on keeping his window open. Protests proved unavailing, and the passengers, left to their own devices in their hunt for warmth, took to doing congas up and down the aisle and, as a last resort, lit a fire at the rear of the bus. It was suggested that we should set fire to the driver, since he was the cause of our troubles in the first place, but it seemed a pointless exercise, since he was well lit up already.

DAN DAREWAYS

Prior to coming to Shetland, I had only flown twice in my life; on both occasions, strangely enough, I did it in aeroplanes. During the first year or so we worked what the company called a bachelor shift pattern, which meant those of us who lived in the British mainland had two breaks per month. The company used a charter air service flying a machine called a Bandierante.

I don't like flying; every time I get into a plane it crosses my mind that I am entering a machine weighing upwards of fifty tons which is expected to defy gravity. The thing that really scared me about the Bandierante was its country of origin; it was manufactured in Brazil.

As far as I knew the Brazilians were good at making coffee and chopping down trees. Their expertise in the aeronautical field was an unknown quantity, and the prospect of proving Newton's theory to be a load of crap, using a machine built by guys dressed in sombreros and flip-flops, and probably shooting cocaine to boot, was less than appealing.

We travelled south for our first leave after a night-shift, and I hoped vainly that I would be too tired to be terrified. The appearance of the aircraft did little to instil confidence; it was so small that the only thing which it appeared to lack was a key to wind it up. The cabin space had a very intimate atmosphere; when filled with passengers it was like a sardine can without the oil.

I got myself an aisle seat next to Angus MacDonald, who fell asleep as soon as we boarded, too early to get the wee morale-boosting speech about emergency exits and lifejackets. We got off the ground and the pilot came over the tannoy, boasting that we were flying at twenty thousand feet and doing two hundred and fifty knots. It occurred to me that at that height and that speed both emergency exits and lifejackets are as much use as a third hump on a camel.

Shortly afterwards the stewardess came round with the coffee. She asked me if MacDonald wanted one, but since he was even less *compos mentis* than usual, I declined on his behalf. She handed me a cup of boiling black coffee, I failed to catch it, and it upended itself in MacDonald's lap.

He was still doubled in agony when he came back to work a week later.

Another problem associated with flying was the uncertainty of the

"Disnae exactly inspire ye wi' confidence, does it, Shug?"

weather; there was never any guarantee that the plane would get off the ground when it was supposed to. The prospect of delay in getting off on leave was always a cause for concern and, during a particularly windy spell, two Soothmoothers, anxious to get back into the arms – or whatever – of their loved ones, decided that, rather than risk the plane, they would book on the ferry. This wasn't exactly inspired thinking; even if it took off late, the aircraft journey time was about two hours to Edinburgh, whereas the boat took fourteen hours to reach Aberdeen.

Nothing daunted, the two caught the boat, which left on time, as did the plane. Unfortunately, there the coincidence ended; the plane arrived on time, but the boat was delayed by a swell which prevented it crossing the bar at Aberdeen harbour, and the two mariners spent the best part of two days cruising up and down the mouth of the Dee.

TECHNOLOGY FOR BEGINNERS

Shortly after first oil ashore, I transferred from jetties to offsites, and returned to the TCC. Despite being at the hub of the alleged Rolls Royce of oil terminals, the TCC was somewhat lacking in the products of what Harold Wilson had proclaimed as the "White Heat of the Technological Revolution". There were three telephones, one of which was only there to make up the numbers and impress the visitors, and an alarm panel which shrieked madly in the event of a plant failure; this had been encased in a seaboot sock and an old wellington boot to muffle its protests.

Everything was done manually, crude tanks had to be dipped during loading and calibration books were used to work out cargo figures; the only thing hi-tech about the place was the kettle, and it was Taiwanese.

Overseeing our activities were shift inspectors who represented the two pipeline systems; many of them had been brought kicking and screaming out of retirement and were geriatric in the extreme. After a short while a bunch of whizzkids were recruited, mostly from the ranks of the British army, which was having a surplus sale due to the absence of any wars of consequence.

One of the geriatrics, Frank Wright, was himself an old soldier, and had spent the war in a mountain battery in India. The battery was drawn by mules, and it was widely held that Frank proved the reverse of the notion that animals grow to look like their masters, for he was decidedly asinine in both appearance and eating habits. It was rumoured that when the war ended the army had got mixed up, given the mule a demob suit and a ticket home, and sent the real Frank to the glue factory.

Frank's major failing was mathematics. The company had seen fit to provide him with a calculator, but Frank, who had never mastered the abacus, found the calculator equally daunting. Unfortunately, a major part of his job was to work out daily stock figures for oil received and exported, a function that was carried out after midnight each night.

By three in the morning Frank would be muttering mild obscenities under his breath, stabbing frantically at the calculator buttons; by five he would be purple with rage and frustration, and at six he would leap to his feet, haul open the door and throw the calculator into the middle distance, following it with a stream of ex-Indian army imprecations which suggested that, by inventing such an infernal machine, the Japanese were getting their own back at him for screwing up their Greater Asian Co-prosperity Sphere in 1945.

Relief for Frank was at hand, however, when one of the whizz-kids was posted to his shift to learn the job. The new recruit was a Boy Wonder of the first order; he was doing so many Open University courses that he had a university to himself. (This surfeit of genius, however, did not prevent him taking a day off work to sit an examination which had taken place the day before!)

Frank spent some time explaining the intricacies of the job, then came to the subject of the midnight figures. "I'll do them," exclaimed the Boy Wonder. "It'll be a piece of cake!"

This suited Frank down to the ground and he told Boy Wonder what was required. "What do you do with the figures when they're finished?" asked Boy Wonder.

"Phone them through to the boss at home," said Frank.

Boy Wonder began punching calculator buttons as if his life depended upon it, while Frank settled back with a copy of *Penthouse*, which he only bought for the cartoons. When it became obvious that Boy Wonder was about to finish the stock sheets, Frank lay back in his chair and feigned sleep; this was easy for him, his problem was feigning wakefulness.

A few minutes later Boy Wonder had finished, and phoned his boss's number to give him the information. Frank's eye clicked open, and a slow smile spread across his face.

"Hello, Adam," said Boy Wonder. "This is James...I've got the midnight figures for you...what time is it?...quarter to three by my watch..."

There was a disbelieving screech from the other end, followed by a stream of invective directed at Boy Wonder, and a resounding crash as the phone came down.

Boy Wonder sat numbly staring at the silent receiver, and suddenly became conscious of Frank's barely muffled chortlings.

"You set me up!" he shouted accusingly.

"No, I didn't," said Frank. "You asked me what I did when I finished the figures and I told you...but I never get them finished before quarter to eight!"

DIVERSIONS

Off duty bevvying was the norm at Staneyhill, and this sort of exercise was seldom carried out in moderation. One night I made the mistake of going out for a blooterfest with Norman Walton, and we wended our way back to Staneyhill about three o'clock in the morning, hanging on to one another for mutual support and promising undying loyalty in the time-honoured fashion. When we got back to the camp Norman fumbled with the lock for a couple of minutes before muttering, "Oh dash it, golly, the lock's jammed!" or words to that effect.

This concerned me a great deal – there was a strong perception that Norman's sex drive was both overpowering and random in its choice of subject, and rumours abounded about a relationship with a site cat on the night-shifts. Apart from anything else, the prospect of sharing a room with his feet was out of the question, so I decided that drastic measures were in order. I stepped back across the corridor and charged at his door.

"Wait a minute," said he, as I hurtled through the woodwork, "I don't think this is my room..."

Which was self evident, since the occupant of the room was cowering in his bed, his eyes out like organ stops.

We got movies once a week on a Wednesday, shown by a prehistoric member of the training department who had been pulled out of retirement. Rab Stoner saw himself as the Staneyhill Morale Officer, but his movies were of the sort now shown at three o'clock in the morning to send insomniacs to bed and to keep Samaritans awake. It was at Staneyhill that I learned the meaning of the term 'cult film', for cult films were the

Morale Officer's speciality. Cult films are usually filmed by Mongolians, with Fijian dialogue, Armenian sub-titles and a plot nearly as comprehensible as a Greek telephone directory.

"You'll like this one," Rab would drool, "it's really sexy..."

Sure enough, there would be a twenty-minute sequence in glorious colour of a couple of yaks going hard at it in a Kathmandu farmyard, or a Yorkshire terrier swinging lustfully on someone's leg.

It was hardly surprising we drank.

About the only thing worth looking forward to was leave, and fortunately we got plenty of that. Leaving luggage lying about on the night before a

"A ventriloquist's dummy, indeed...must be a ventriloquist's convention in Shetland..that's the fourth one on the Sullom Voe flight this week..."

flight was, however, a risky business; one traveller arrived in Cardiff totally exhausted, and only discovered on opening his luggage that his workmates had complemented his load of dirty socks and underwear with a couple of bricks.

Even more unfortunate was a representative from a cleaning company which had the contract for cleaning offices and control rooms on site. The charladies employed by this outfit were on the whole far removed from the traditional image of the species, and were frequently the objects of lustful gropings from the lower classes in the site control rooms. The representative had dealt somewhat brusquely with their claim for higher wages and had got up their noses in a big way.

When he arrived at the airport his luggage was subject to the usual security check and he was most discomfited when the security guard pulled a large artificial male organ from the bottom of his case and asked politely, but loudly enough to draw the attention of all around:

"Does this appliance have batteries in it, sir?"

SNOW, SNOW, THICK THICK SNOW

Over the years much of what was said at recruitment interviews has been forgotten, but the statement which stuck in the minds of all those who came from south to Sullom Voe was, "It never snows in Shetland, and when it does, it doesn't lie."

Very cold rain started falling on Hogmanay 1978, and drifted to depths of six feet; it was still lying on the hills, looking suspiciously like snow to anyone cynical enough to doubt the company's honesty, in April the following year.

Shetland Islands Council owned two snow-ploughs, one of which took fright and seized up when it saw the enormity of the task in front of it. The other struggled manfully through the white hell until it encountered a BP manager driving a Range Rover who, as it turned out, was a kamikaze afficionado, and managed to write off both vehicles.

Our shift was unlucky enough to be marooned in Lerwick on New Year's morning; rather than sit about Staneyhill waiting for the weather to get better we decided to accept the chef's invitation to visit his house for a wee boozefest.

The celebrations flowed with much merriment and imbibement, to the extent that after an hour or so Wee Joe lapsed into a Grouse induced coma. There was some debate about what should be done with him, and eventually we put him into one of the bedrooms to sleep it off, since the hamster cage was already occupied.

Shortly afterwards two Guizers appeared; it is a tradition in Shetland for the male of the species to dress up in female garments at New Year and wander the streets. (This form of diversion would get you room and board in a police station anywhere else in the UK.) Both of them were wearing masks, and one was particularly grotesque. About four o'clock in the morning we decided to take our leave, and sent the ugly Guizer into the bedroom to arouse wee Joe from his slumbers.

Wee Joe's screams could be heard three streets away, and it took us half an hour to unpick him from the ceiling.

Even more unlucky was the shift which we should have relieved, which did about three days without a break. The company was extravagant with its thanks until some mercenary suggested a wee bung as a reward for devotion above and beyond the call of duty wouldn't go amiss; the limits of the company's extravagance became quickly apparent.

At first the snow brought novelty value; pornographic snowmen dotted the Staneyhill landscape, and a favourite trick was to wait until a victim had settled himself into the toilet trap with a copy of the *Readers' Digest Book of Great Toilets,* and heave a bucket of snow over the partition; this was a sure cure for constipation and was guaranteed to fuse pacemakers.

Eventually, however, the arctic weather brought problems to the happy campers of Staneyhill, since all the pipes froze and left us without water. The manager had conveniently taken himself off on holiday at the start of the crisis, leaving us in the hands of the chef, an Irishman with a strange sense of humour and an even stranger standard of cuisine. His maxim was that he made mistakes and we ate them; he always laughed as he said it, which made him look remarkably like a praying mantis about to devour its victim.

Eating camp food during the freeze became even more fraught with hazard than usual. The toilets were also frozen and the inmates had to brave the elements and relieve themselves outside. The chef was melting snow for cooking purposes, and after a few days it was difficult to find snow which was not of the yellow variety. When green pea soup appeared on the menu three days in succession there was a mass exodus to the Happy Haddock chippie.

After about a week there was no sign of an improvement in the position, and life at Staneyhill was getting decidedly odiferous. The emergency committee was convened, and it was unanimously approved – with two abstentions – that two delegates be sent to the Managerial Mansion, then sited in the Lerwick Hotel, to convey the disapproval of the inmates. The two abstentions were nominated as delegates, the logic being that they were by far the oldest inmates, and had less to lose by being sacked.

We had chosen our representatives well; the elder of the pair, by about three centuries, was Ben Butler, who favoured a natty line in lacy underwear and supported Fulham, which is more than enough aberrations to be going on with. His partner, Jack Hornsea, came from Hartlepool; he was notable in having legs like a chicken wishbone, so widely spaced that even a Scottish international striker could have put a ball through them. The good burghers of Hartlepool put their town on the map during the Napoleonic wars when they captured a shipwrecked monkey and hung it as a suspected French spy; there was a conviction among the Staneyhill intelligentsia that Jack was the reincarnation of the victim of this miscarriage of justice.

Having been duly elected to air the grievances of their comrades to the Godfathers, the delegates concluded that it was unlikely they would get a Prime Ministerial reception of beer and sandwiches, and therefore stoked up to excess with the former in a Lerwick hostelry prior to carrying out their mission. With a substantial cargo aboard, they went to the reception of the hotel, and were informed that Mr Seaman was in his room.

The delegates, by now in a sufficiently aggressive mood to take on the Red Army, knocked on the Corporate Servant's door, and were somewhat taken aback when Mr Seaman appeared clad in a towel.

"Sorry to keep you waiting," said he, "I was just having a bath." This, in the circumstances, was not a very diplomatic opening line, and Ben's ire rose to danger level.

"Good for you mate," he snarled, "We haven't had water, never mind bath water, for a week. Why don't you put your clothes on and come and have a look?"

Mr Seaman was profuse in his condolences, and invited his visitors to wait until he had changed, pointedly locking the cocktail cabinet as he went into his bedroom.

Ten minutes later the delegates returned to Staneyhill with their hostage, who had been subjected to severe stereophonic GBH on route about the company's indifference to the plight of its servants.

When the trio entered the accommodation block it was to find the bathrooms full of steam and the inmates showering en masse; the water had come on five minutes after their departure, and the search party sent to waylay the delegation in order to prevent their embarrassment had gone to the wrong pub.

"Hell, Fred, I didn't realise it was that cold..."

There was a lot of movement in and out of Staneyhill as the sub-zero winter turned to a sub-zero spring. More new starts were arriving daily, other new starts were staying just long enough to get other jobs elsewhere, and others were moving to houses at Firth and Brae, two newly-built housing estates near the terminal. The camp population dwindled rapidly as the available housing stock increased, but the few long-term survivors displayed a marked reluctance to take the plunge and move their families up.

There was little question that one or two little omissions from the recruitment brochure had come to light and given the would-be immigrants cause for second thoughts.

For a start, Shetland weather patterns are unique. In the first year there were five seasons; four of them were winter and the fifth was utterly hellish. Hurricane force winds and horizontal rain seemed to be the norm, sheep were nailed to the fields to stop them blowing away, and standard beachwear in the summer was parkas and sweaters.

The landscape, too, was alien to those from an urban environment. It was relatively flat and treeless, and the north mainland seemed to be one vast peat bog. There was also the prospect of a fourteen-hour boat trip to reach the nearest branch of Marks and Spencer, a voyage not for the faint-hearted in a North Sea winter.

Despite being allocated a house, I was reluctant to move up; those who had made the move were bemoaning conditions on the new estates. The houses had been built somewhat hastily – according to rumour, construction time was three hours ten minutes per dwelling, including a half-hour mealbreak – and were causing problems to their residents. The Brae estate was nicknamed Toytown, and it was alleged that the houses designed to house five people were only suitable as hutches for single undernourished rabbits. This, coupled with the almost total lack of shopping facilities in the area, did not endear the area to the newcomers, most of whom were used to the conveniences of a metropolitan environment.

The notion of paying three times the norm for tomatoes which were three years past their sell-by date was anathema, and this was compounded by the rather cavalier attitude encapsulated in the encounter between an English immigrant and a local shopkeeper, when the former went into the shop to order his *Radio Times*. His request was refused on the grounds that the shopkeeper already had far too many orders for papers.

There was, however, some pressure on me from the wife, usually around the windpipe, and in April 1979, I conceded defeat and got myself and my family domesticated in Shetland.

THE NEW SHETLANDER

Our new residence was in Mossbank, and masqueraded under the nom-de-plume of a chalet-bungalow; the same type of structure built in 1945 would have been called a prefab. It had all the inbuilt extras which came free of charge with the houses on the estate: doors which wouldn't shut, windows which wouldn't open, and a combined drainage and sewerage system which turned the garden into an ocean of second-hand Delsey every time it rained.

The builder's parting shot, however, was the walk-in cupboards under the eaves. Anyone walking in would immediately descend with terminal velocity into the living room below, since the cupboards lacked floorboards. Quite a few houses had their own running water, having been built directly over streams which expanded to rivers every time it rained.

The houses had a toilet and a bathroom; logically one would have been on the upper floor and the other on the ground floor, but they were in fact next to one another, as a result of which – failing an outbreak of dysentery – the toilet was seldom used. One entrepreneur took the door off his toilet, covered the doorway with wire mesh, and filled the space with budgies.

The real *pièce de résistance*, however, was the heating system, which was obviously designed to enrich the Hydro Board. There is no mains gas in Shetland, despite the fact that Sullom Voe processes vast quantities of propane and butane; the new estates were all fitted with electric panel heaters, which are about as efficient as a coal-fired Concorde.

This, combined with an almost total lack of insulation, meant that in winter the houses were, to all intents and purposes, five-apartment fridge freezers, and the only thing which was hot was the electricity meter; it was advisable to play a hose on it to prevent it from bursting into flames. Winter in the Mossbank Gulag was not going to be a fun event.

The estates were a strange environment, full of incomers and lacking the mix of a normal society. The average age of residents was probably around thirty-five, and this in itself was a destabilising influence, since in most cases grandparents and other older relatives were still on the British mainland.

There was a considerable social whirl in the early days; the lack of facilities meant that house parties were the norm. We were invited one evening to a small soirée at Joe Bryant's house which went on into the small hours. About half past twelve I staggered home and paid off the baby-sitter. The rug rats were all fast asleep and I returned to the party, intending to check every fifteen minutes or so to make sure all was well.

The problem with getting around Mossbank is that the quickest way around is between houses, rather than using roads or footpaths; the disadvantage is that all the houses came out of the same box and they all look identical. I made a couple of trips back to the humble abode, stumbling through the mire in the darkness, and on the third trip I arrived at the house to see the front room light on and the silhouette of a head in the window. I went through the front door like a New York cop on a drugs bust and hurtled into the front room at twenty knots, shouting, "What the hell are you doing out of your bed?"

Straight into a room full of strangers in the house in the next block.

SEA FEVER

The first priority among those moving from the mainland was the purchase of a boat; the quantum leap in the small boat market resulted in astute Shetlanders disposing of, for vast prices, vessels which were incapable of keeping rainwater in, far less keeping the ocean out.

My next door neighbour, Mark Byrnes, was quickly infected by an urge to go down to the sea in ships. He went forth and purchased a

"You'll love sailing, you said...fresh air and relaxation you said... good for the kids you said...will you stop whipping Cedric with that rope..."

Seagull outboard, which is, as any weekend mariner will affirm, a remarkably reliable means of propelling small boats. To complement it, however, Mark chose an inflatable dinghy which had the proportions and seakeeping qualities of a leaky airbed.

He launched this ensemble, containing his wife, children, and two cases of lager, into the waters of Yell Sound which, even on a summer's day, has tide rips that make the Corrievreckan seem like a ripple. He managed, however, to do a round tour of various islands without mishap, and brought his family back safely. On disembarking with the outboard, alas, Mark missed the jetty and hit the sea, disappearing into twenty fathoms of water like a crash-diving submarine. His rate of descent was accelerated considerably by his reluctance to let go the outboard, which had cost him a lot of money, and this pecuniary fixation gave him the buoyancy of an anchor.

Two intrepid mariners decided to take their dinghy for some fishing in the waters off the island of Bressay, and were on the point of returning when they discovered their outboard had broken down, and they couldn't make any headway against the ebb tide. The skipper was, however, well equipped and decided to call for help with a flare. This was, in itself, commendably sensible, but his method of setting it off was somewhat unorthodox, for he held it against his chest and pulled the string. As a result he set his parka ablaze, while the flare itself, instead of soaring into the heavens, disappeared somewhat ineffectually up his left nostril.

THE NEW WORLD

There was little question that life in Shetland was going to be different; it was far removed from the rest of Scotland in more than just distance.

It had its own council, from whose chambers emanated some real gems of wisdom. One individual, for instance, displayed an excess of humanitarian zeal during a debate on nuclear weapons by stating that he was:

"...glad that the bomb had been dropped on Hiroshima, since it meant he didn't need to go to Burma with the army..."

A debate on the extension of an island graveyard, which averaged an interment once a year, was enlivened when a sage pointed out that this should not engender complacency since "there might be a plague". His fellow members bowed to this gem of wisdom and agreed that the matter be given top priority.

After Strathclyde, this standard of professional excellence was a breath of fresh air...

In one issue of the local paper there was a request from the police for witnesses to an accident in which a pedestrian had been knocked down by a car.

The following issue contained a postscript to the effect that the pedestrian had not, in fact, been knocked down by the car; he had been lying in the road when the car hit him.

The most inspired use of communication, however, had to be the outside broadcast, transmitted by Radio Shetland's sports correspondent to its spellbound listeners, of an indoor cricket match.

To ensure that nothing would detract from the excitement and drama of the game, not a single word of commentary was spoken during the ten-minute broadcast; the only sounds which broke the silence of the airwaves were the sounds of the ball hitting the bat, the scuffle of running feet, and the occasional ecstatic "Howzat!"

THE MISSING HEIRLOOM

The housing manager finally cracked when the redoubtable Muff Hutchins decided to move his family to Shetland. Muff's wife was a demure damsel with some musical talent; apart from being a virtuoso with the spoons, she had been a long serving member of the Ardrossan Loyal Orange Order Flute Band, and could sing "The Sash My Father Wore" with enough pathos to bring tears to the eyes of the Pope himself. At that time they were blessed with one child, Minimuff, who was a miniature version of her father; at three years old her vocabulary stretched to around ten words, all of which were culled from the seamier bits of *Lady Chatterley's Lover*.

Muff's removal went without a hitch, except for the fact that somewhere along the way his chip pan went adrift. Since the Clan Muff subsisted on nothing else, the risk of impending famine impelled Muff to telephone the housing officer at two in the morning. He explained that the chip pan was a priceless and irreplaceable family heirloom, and demanded an immediate search should be mounted to recover it. For about a week the hapless Company Servant was bombarded with calls about the missing item and eventually, after he had telephoned just about every house in the neighbourhood, the priceless artefact turned up in Angus MacDonald's house, having mysteriously switched removal vans en route.

The housing officer put in an immediate demand to return to sea. The company, in recognition of his heroic performance at Sullom Voe, posted him to an Iranian tanker on charter to BP, which went to the Gulf and promptly got itself plastered by an Iraqi missile. There was a strong

rumour that the Iraqis had been fed inside information by those un-
fortunates who had been allocated houses by the tanker's radio officer.

THE WILD ROVER

One thing that Mossbank had in abundance was dogs. We had brought an old Shetland cross with us from the mainland and shortly after we arrived got a collie setter cross pup called Trooker. Trooker made friends with another dog of indeterminate origin called Ben, whose party trick was to open the front door, flush the toilet, and go back out again. Trooker was not slow to pick up his tricks, and in a very short time could open not just the doors, but the windows as well.

The canine stud of the district was an animal called Rusty, who certainly wasn't corroded where it mattered. Rusty was, however, totally indiscriminate in his sexual tastes; this was borne out by the number of barking cats and sheep in the neighbourhood.

There were, however, certain residents who viewed Rusty's courtship of their dogs with disfavour.

One resident in particular had two Shetland sheepdog bitches whose pedigree went back to Bannockburn, and was hoping to breed them when they came into season.

He had neglected to tell Rusty, however, that he wasn't included in the choice of breeding partners, and the lady of the house was horrified to come out one morning to find Rusty and one of the bitches giving it big licks in the garden.

She eventually managed to extricate her bitch from Rusty's embrace, and hustled it into the car, intending to take it to the vet to inhibit it producing Rusty's offspring.

When she had regained her composure she was relieved to see that Rusty had gone; unfortunately, so had her other Shetland sheepdog.

What remained of her composure disintegrated when she received a phone call a few minutes later to tell her that Rusty was giving Gung Ho to her other bitch a couple of blocks away.

Rusty's perambulations continued when he made the acquaintance of a Cavalier King Charles spaniel bitch. This aristocrat lived in a kennel outside, and the canine Casanova soon had his wicked way with her, to the owner's acute displeasure.

He made an appointment with the vet, who had bought a holiday villa in Marbella on the strength of repairing the consequences of Rusty's misdemeanours, and decided to use the time before going to the vet constructing defences around his dog's kennel.

After about four hours' work his garden looked like Fort Apache, completely shut off by a massive fence about twelve feet high which kept out everything, including the light to the house.

"Has that damn dog of yours got <u>any</u> moral scruples?"

Having completed his task, he took his dog for her termination. He was less that pleased on his return to find Rusty, panting in anticipation, sitting in the kennel.

The operations superintendent, he who had delivered unto the masses his interpretation of First Oil Ashore, owned a huge English sheepdog called Digby, which was in fact a mobile des. res. for about ten generations of fleas. He – the dog, not the operations superintendent – bore more than a passing resemblance to a doormat, and was wont to bite the leg off unwary souls who tried to use him as one.

Not content with being saddled with this oversize canine Godzilla, Alf also owned a pet sheep called Fred which, it was rumoured, spoke better English than he did. Fred wandered the estate looking for dogs to play with, totally ignoring the vast flocks of his fellow tribesmen who inhabited the area. His confusion was probably furthered by the fact that he was a ewe.

One day Trooker decided to invite Fred into our house for a meal in my absence, and I returned to find that the guest had scoffed a tin of Chappie, a packet of cornflakes, and a jumbo pack of washing up powder.

The result of this cocktail on Fred's bowels can be imagined; when I came into the kitchen she was standing up to her hollyhocks in steaming ordure with – naturally – a sheepish expression on her face.

THE TAFFIA

Changes were fast and furious in the early days; having got oil ashore, there was a big push to get the gas processing plant on stream to provide more shekels for the corporate coffers. There was, however, considerable discontent in the ranks, which spread from the fire department into operations, and soon the majority of the lower orders had joined a trade union, and the company was pressured to afford recognition.

To cope with the problem of dealing with the revolution among the Great Unwashed, the company imported a new creation, an industrial relations officer.

Sullom Voe was already polluted with a variety of specimens of the *dai bach* brigade, known to the lower orders as the Taffia; the terminal manager, operations manager, and operations superintendent all sounded like a cross between the late lamented Hilda Ogden and a Pakistani bus conductor with laryngitis.

Despite what was widely perceived as a surfeit of the tribe, the new industrial relations officer, Jim Cockell, turned out to be yet another one, leading to speculation that somewhere in company headquarters there were rows of Welshmen in little boxes ready for despatch to Sullom Voe.

It dawned on us very quickly that the new Taff had evolved empty Welsh rhetoric into a form which would have been eligible for an Arts Council grant. He and the operations manager, a rotund character called Ray Colman, were a superb double act, although they were more Burke and Hare than Abbott and Costello. It was generally considered that if Jim Cockell, rather than Brutus, had delivered the eulogy over the body of Caesar, both the audience and the corpse would have gone home before he had finished.

After one particularly inspired peroration, a notice appeared, albeit briefly, above the button on the hot air hand dryer in the administration block toilet exhorting staff to "press here for a sixty second speech by Jim Cockell".

The duo were aided and abetted in negotiation by the emergency services superintendent, Richard Anster, who was yet another of the tribe. His forte was big words; when the other two were short on answers – or on breath, which was more often the case – Richard would fill the breach with a stream of long, impressive, and generally unconnected big words.

This had the desired effect, since it brought any sensible discussion to an abrupt halt while the union side adjourned to work out what the hell he was talking about. We once phoned the Transport and General HQ in Aberdeen to find out what 'deleterious' meant.

The terminal manager, Doctor Harkins, was a remarkably pleasant chap, despite his nationality. He had an incredible knack of being able to put names to faces, which was very disconcerting for such as myself, who subscribe to the view that anonymity is an ideal cloak for chronic incompetence.

He made a practice of wandering about the plant when any self-respecting dayworker should have been busy on extra-mural activities like playing golf or engaging in a little canine knowledge with another consenting adult. As a result, he was liable to appear in control rooms in the middle of heavy brag schools or the formal opening of a consignment of highly erudite Swedish literature from a visiting tanker.

On one occasion a contractor cut himself on site, and was advised by his supervisor that, rather than bleed to death in the firm's time, he should go for medical treatment. The casualty's grasp of the terminal's geography, however, was somewhat vague, and he was unable to find the medical centre. Being blessed with considerable initiative, however, he checked the telephone directory for a suitable person to treat his wounds, as a result of which Doctor Harkins had a surprise visitor, bleeding all over his carpet, who demanded to be stitched up. He pointed out to the would-be patient that his degree in chemical engineering from Yabba Dabba Doo University hadn't covered elementary needlework.

The power station also had an obligatory Welshman whose mission in life was to educate the planet. This he did by a vast outpouring of memos, which swiftly engulfed the site in a morass of paperwork, expounding his wisdom on a variety of subjects ranging from the quality of canteen mince to the design of gas turbines. Unfortunately his literary verbosity was such that it was difficult to distinguish whether he was suggesting redesigning the inlet valves on the mince or using garlic instead of onions to improve the efficiency of the turbines.

He was matched by the Assistant Oil and Gas Loss Accountant, whose misfortune it was to share an office with the Oil Movements Superintendent. This unfortunate, also a Blod, was required to accompany his superior to the local hostelry and match him pint for pint in consuming lakes of strong drink.

After a few months of this his grasp of reality became somewhat blurred and a fit of spontaneous erudition resulted in the following memo appearing on site noticeboards:

"The quantity of oil allocated to the Brent and Ninian systems in any one month will equal the percentage but will not necessarily be equivalent to the quantity of oil recovered in that month."

His talent was immediately recognised and he was promoted and posted to Britain.

ASBESTOS MAN

The terminal had three distinct groups: Them, us, and the fire department, which was an entity of its own. It was a uniform department with a local authority rank structure and enough equipment to put out the Great Fire of London in about ten minutes flat. It seemed to us that each member of the department had at least one vehicle, and the fact that most of the terminal's budget seemed to be directed towards preparing for Armageddon was less than conducive to good morale.

The officers took their role remarkably seriously; the firemaster was stopped by the police and told to remove the red light from the top of his car. This was not surprising in view of the fact that he was on his way to the West Country on holiday, and was on the M6 just north of Preston at the time.

The uniform of senior officers, who seemed to outnumber other ranks by about two to one, had allegedly been designed by one of the said officers, and gave the wearer the appearance of a downmarket Ruritanian field marshal; there was little question that power went to the head of the wearer when clad in this ensemble, and it was strongly rumoured that the terminal manager only stopped in time a plot to issue officers with sidearms.

The department was the source of much speculation, primarily because its senior officers seemed to have an unfortunate tendency to get into embarrassing situations. During one week the fire chief managed to sink his Range Rover in a quagmire, and was quickly upstaged by his deputy, Roy Parrish, who took a member of the local constabulary on a site tour, made a navigational blunder, and submerged his Landrover in a flooded tank bund. Within hours, the terminal noticeboards carried an advertisement showing a Landrover fording a stream, with the legend: "To a car, it's a river; to a Landrover, it's a road," to which had been added: "To Roy, it's an embarrassment."

The ranking structure was rigid indeed. Two firemen, hiking along the road in driving rain, were relieved when a car stopped alongside them; their assistant firemaster poked his head out of the window and said, "Sorry, lads, I'd give you a lift, but I'm an officer!" before driving off to leave them to hope that the next vehicle might be driven by a member of the proletariat.

It will be obvious from the foregoing that rank and grey matter in the terminal fire department did not necessarily go hand in hand; one officer took up birdwatching and announced to the lower echelons that he had spent an afternoon on the island of Unst watching squadrons of penguins gliding about the heavens, while another carried out an impromptu test on a fire extinguisher in his Landrover, and it was only a thick coating of white powder which hid his blushes from his chortling minions. The minions too had their share of balloons; one had shipped on the *Queen Mary* as a fireman and demonstrated his engineering expertise by filling the tourist class swimming pool with fuel oil, and ensured his early discharge by inadvertently throwing the chief engineer's Sunday bunnet into the furnace.

The fire department were not called out often, but when they were they tended to come out in force. The slightest hint of a problem brought them thundering onto the roads of the terminal like a motorised Seventh Cavalry, lights flashing and klaxons blaring. One celebrated occasion arose from a construction worker being marooned in a faulty overhead crane in the crude loading meter shed; the supervisor on duty decided that the only way to retrieve the individual was to have the fire department send up their schnorkel wagon and have him brought down, and he telephoned the fire station control room to request that this be done.

Seconds later the air was rent with the shrieks of the fire brigade's vehicles, pouring out of the station house in full force, carrying troops kitted out to the eyeballs with breathing apparatus and fire axes. This display of professionalism on the move would have been more impressive had they known where they were going; the would-be recipient of their attentions was somewhat discomfited when they roared past the crude loading meters and went instead to the crude pumphouse half a mile away.

The regard in which the fire department was held was illustrated one evening in the restaurant, on the occasion of the birthday of one of the fire control room girls, a rather luscious creature.

As she came in for her meal, the fire shift gave a spirited rendering of "Happy Birthday".

At the end of the chorus there was a loud stage whisper from a nearby table:

"God help us if she's got a birthday cake...they'll never put the candles out..."

There was still plenty of manna for the masses in these days, although in early 1980 the free boozefests began to tail off. Come November, however, the company invested money in fireworks with enough gunpowder content to wipe the archipelago off the map, and very nearly succeeded. A display was planned at the Brae Sailing Club, the haunt of the Higher Echelons, to be overseen by the operations manager, who would receive technical advice from a pyrotechnics specialist from the terminal's fire department. With such a wealth of alleged professionalism to hand, it would seem safe to assume that all eventualities would be catered for.

The best laid plans of mice and men, however, went agley in a big way when the operations manager, showing incredible ineptitude – even by company standards – lit the first firework and promptly dropped it in the box containing the rest of the high explosive. This concerned him somewhat, and he turned to ask the advice of the intrepid firefighter, only to find him legging it into the distance, screaming at the top of his voice: "Take cover! Hide under your beds...board up your windows... don't panic...Oh, my God...we're all doomed!"

The explosion made quite a mess, mostly of the operations superintendent, who required nearly half a roll of Delsey to regain his composure.

Guy Fawkes, wherever he is, must have been hysterical.

RINGING THE CHANGES

In the early eighties there was an exodus of some magnitude to another oil company whose recruiters had an even more convincing line of patter than BP. The exodus included our supervisor and shift foreman.

The supervisor was replaced by a diminutive character, on whose head a safety helmet looked like a garden hut and gave him more than a passing resemblance to a nail. He was promptly dubbed The Hat.

Like all small men, he was aggressive, and spent his spare time roaming the moors with a large shotgun, blasting the rabbit population into oblivion. He kept a number of large dogs, and his penchant for deerstalker bunnets soon earned him the sobriquet Laird of Voe.

On the whole he was no more anti-social than any other member of the supervisory staff (which gave him plenty of latitude), apart from his delusion that he was blessed with musical talent. The fact that he chose to express this alleged talent with bagpipes did little to enhance his relations with his neighbours, and these deteriorated rapidly to Arab-Israeli standards when he decided to open boarding kennels. The irate residents, already assailed by the tortured wails of The Hat's musical enemas, immediately queued up to oppose planning permission for his canine Holiday Inn. Not to be outdone in the anti-social stakes, Hat did his homework and put it about the neighbourhood that, while he did need planning permission for kennels, there was no such restriction on breeding pigs in his front room or opening a locust hatchery.

Our shift foreman, Norman, moved on just in time to escape a deluge of richly deserved retribution from all quarters, and was replaced by the Welshman who had carried the bricks home to Cardiff. He proved to be a true professional, which might have been what we needed, but certainly wasn't what we wanted. His promotion came out of the blue, and was greeted somewhat less than enthusiastically by his new subordinates.

The problem was that, not only could he remember the bricks we had put in his luggage, he also remembered the occasion when he had been caught short on the bus home and had got off to relieve himself, at which point his fellow passengers had persuaded the driver to pull away.

The human anatomy is not designed to cope with trying to relieve oneself while running sideways at thirty miles per hour. The victim of the shift's somewhat perverse sense of humour now found himself in a position to exact revenge on the perpetrators.

As a result of the promotions the oldest operator on our shift was elevated to control room operator, on the supposed basis of his vast experience in the industry, but in reality because one Shetland winter on the plant had afflicted him with every disease known to man, and a few from extra-terrestrial sources.

A Mastermind candidate he assuredly was not; he had once rented a video of *Watership Down* under the misapprehension that it was about the war in the Pacific, and complained bitterly to the shop owner that someone had wiped the film and substituted a cartoon about rabbits, and it didn't even have the saving grace of Bugs Bunny in the cast. The senior control room operator was even worse; he suffered from chronic dyslexia – he insisted that his food had to be properly masturbated before he would swallow it – and could mutilate even words of one syllable into total incomprehensibility.

In 1981 a group of trainee operators began on the terminal, and we got one on our shift. Willie Frater was six feet tall and must have weighed nearly four stones with his parka on. He also sported long bushy hair, and bore a striking resemblance to a cotton bud with a perm. On his first nightshift the shift foreman asked him to go to the tank farm, over a mile away, and run some checks; since it was raining, he told him to take a van. Five minutes later, Willie staggered into the control room with his glasses in the Eric Morecambe mode, his face totally devoid of blood. "I've crashed the van outside," he wailed.

It's amazing how quickly good news travels; within five minutes there were about fifty people standing around the remains of the van. Remains they certainly were, and the van was undoubtedly bound for the great garage in the sky. The entrance to the car park was at least twenty feet wide; Willie had missed it completely and piled the van into a drainage culvert.

The foreman was not pleased. "Where the hell did you learn to drive?" he exploded, eyeing Willie's handiwork.

"I didn't..." replied Willie glumly.

"You mean you can't drive?" the foreman asked incredulously. "Why the hell didn't you tell me?"

Willie's answer was crushing in its logic. "You never asked," he said calmly.

At the same time the fire department also got a batch of trainees. The prospect of suddenly earning megabucks went to the head of one new start, who invested about ten years' salary in a huge motor cruiser; this despite the fact that his house was devoid of carpets.

Shortly after he started on shift he asked for a night off, and was told that he could have it, as long as he got a mate to cover for him.

Sure enough, on the night in question the fire shift mustered for duty, exuding a totally misleading air of professional competence in their uniforms. Standing out like a sore thumb at the end of the front rank was a seedy individual in jeans and a leather jacket, festooned in chains and Iron Crosses.

"Who the hell are you?" enquired the station officer.

"I'm Tommy's mate," said the apprentice Hell's Angel, "You said he should get a mate to cover him so that he could have the night off."

On his return to work, Tommy was taken gently to one side and enlightened on the fact that, should he require cover in the future, the company would prefer that it be done by one of its own employees.

MUFF AND THE CLASS STRUGGLE

The unionisation of the plant was somewhat fraught; there was a perception that the lot of employees had been improved little by union membership. It did, however, result in numerous procedures being formalised, including a disciplinary procedure.

One of the first to fall victim to the disciplinary procedure was Muff, which surprised nobody, since he was somewhat mercurial to say the least. He was working in the stores, but also had a part-time job in a Lerwick booze boutique, where he could be seen most nights taking on pints of export as ballast.

Unfortunately his over-indulgence resulted in frequent absences from work, and his manager made known his displeasure in no uncertain terms. Muff did not like his manager, and paid little attention to the warnings; consequently he soon received an invitation to discuss his future with the company, and was pointedly advised to bring his trade union representative along.

The branch chairman at that time was a former London fireman, and he did not relish the prospect of doing his Perry Mason on Muff's behalf.

They had a pre-meeting outside the manager's office, at which the hapless official tried to co-ordinate Muff's defence, which the defendant had clearly fixed in his mind.

"A clear case of victimisation, so it is, hey...a pure dig oot. He's jist tryin' tae get me because ah can pull the burds an' he cannae because he's goat a puss like a kangaroo's erse so he has..." For reasons best known to himself, this defence, which Muff considered cast iron, did not inspire his counsel.

At that time – remember that Britain still had some industry in the early eighties – the Transport and General Workers' Union had about two million members; Muff, convinced as he was of the solidarity of the working classes, obviously believed that with the masses marching behind him, albeit metaphorically, he could do no wrong.

Fired with the spirit of the class war, Muff marched into the manager's office; he strode up to the desk, banged his fist upon it, stared the representative of Capitalist Exploitation straight in the eye and opened the negotiations with: "Right, ya bastard..."

RAISING THE COLOURS

The unionisation of the plant coincided with the arrival of the most important item of equipment on the terminal, the Flagpole. As usual, it lay in a shed for three months while the engineers designed a hole for it and the planning department held lengthy meetings to decide where to stick it. There were numerous suggestions on the latter from disaffected elements among the lower echelons; most of them were eminently sensible, anatomically implausible, and would have proved extremely painful to the operations manager had they been acted upon. Eventually the great day arrived and the flagpole was duly erected outside the terminal gate. At that point it was discovered that there was no flag to hang upon it; this dilemma was solved by a personnel officer who, despite his profession, showed remarkable initiative and offered to acquire a Union Flag.

This suggestion sent the engineering superintendent, Fred Holt, into a paroxysm of rage. "Ah'll be damned," said he," if yer gonny hing a Transport an' General Workers flag oan that pole!" (He was Scots.)

The indignant company servant was taken gently aside and told that the term "Union Flag" is the correct title for that flag commonly and erroneously known as the Union Jack.

Loyal Company Servants undergo intensive training to curb normal human emotions like compassion and embarrassment; the ability to disguise the latter comes in very useful when offering trade union representatives a two per cent rise the day after the company chairman has awarded himself thirty per cent. Not even his training, however, could save Fred Holt's blushes the night he attended a Hallowe'en party.

Hallowe'en is the one festival in the British calendar during which men can dress as women without an eyebrow being raised, and the party bore more than a passing resemblance to a transvestites' ball; the hall seemed to be filled by large hairy welders mincing around in lacy basques and fishnet stockings, their upper torsos stretched to unlikely proportions by strategically placed balloons.

As the evening wore on, Fred's glow quotient increased dramatically, and he took it upon himself to have a quick grope at the vast balloons of one particularly well endowed Guizer, who appeared to be wearing two zeppelins up his frock. The balloons, however, were remarkably firm, and the unfortunate Fred discovered to his consternation that he was fondling the only real woman in the room.

His apology was less than diplomatic; staggering out of handbag range, he spluttered: "I'm sorry – I thought you were a man!"

AN ACCIDENT WITH FEET

There were few accidents on site, but our shift had one. His name was Magnie Jamieson.

Magnie did not believe in gravity, and shuffled about as if he was wearing skis, never lifting his feet from terra firma; as a result he was liable to trip over just about anything, and did so with incredible frequency. He seldom came to work without battle damage of some sort, and reportedly had a standing appointment with the Lerwick Hospital's casualty department, where generations of surgeons had learned their skills on him.

The fact that this was a talent of long standing came to light when a Sunday newspaper ran a feature requesting wives to tell them how they had first met their husbands.

Sure enough, a letter appeared from Magnie's wife, relating how she was a nurse in hospital in Edinburgh where Magnie had been a patient. Apparently he had been to a party and had performed a back flip and treble somersault down a flight of stairs; this display of athletic prowess had earned him a storm of applause from his fellow guests and a number of substantial dents to his anatomy.

On his release from hospital he had asked his wife out on a date. She had been captivated by his blue eyes, which was just as well, for it's difficult to be a Lothario when your jaw is broken in three places and is held together with more wire than a telephone exchange.

Needless to say, the photocopiers were running on overload producing copies of the famous letter, which was soon appearing on every noticeboard on site, and reappearing just as fast as Magnie could pull them down.

There was much speculation as to the repercussions of all this press coverage in Old Blue Eyes' household, since it was obvious that he felt it was publicity he could do without.

It was, however, impossible for him to hide his talent under a bushel. His *pièce de résistance* was ramming a crude oil tank with the shift van; the tank was fifty yards from the nearest road.

One person on site was unquestionably mad, bad, and dangerous to know, and that was Shagpile MacDonald. I hate having my hair cut, but at one stage my cranium looked more than usually like a burst mattress, and Shagpile volunteered to cut it on the night-shift. He had been snipping away confidently for ten minutes when I asked him if he'd ever done it professionally. "No," he said coolly, "In fact, I've never done it before..."

One summer in the early eighties the waters around Shetland were full of squid; it was impossible to drop a line from a boat without bringing one up. One Friday afternoon they started throwing themselves on to the beach at the terminal, and within a short time there were literally millions of them along about a hundred yards of shoreline. The cause of this phenomenon was unknown, but when our shift came in on night-shift that night the glut of dead squid proved a great temptation. Shagpile got some plastic bags, filled them with deceased squid, and spent the entire shift touring the terminal and planting the corpses. Late squid were nailed under desks, and planted strategically in vehicles whose owners were off for the weekend; the Ninian Range Rover was allocated five cadavers.

By the Monday a bulldozer had cleared the beach, but there was still, in certain areas, a strong and growing odour of disintegrating squid; the last corpse was finally tracked down in a filing cabinet three weeks later.

Shortly after that I swapped houses with Shagpile. He had left a large quantity of assorted ironmongery underneath the floor and it took me some time to figure out what it was.

He had apparently been infected by the Thatcher Enterprise Culture in a big way and had built himself a private distillery.

For months after we moved in I was terrified to open the door in case it was a police raid.

THE BRAINS TRUSSED

The company in its wisdom decided that shift drivers should be recruited; this went down well with the troops since frequently it was difficult to muster enough bodies for a decent game of brag.

We inherited a character straight out of *Eastenders*, who managed to put in more sick time than Lazarus. He was a car enthusiast, and spent his spare time rebuilding perfectly good automobiles into unsightly deathtraps. He also gave Magnie a run for his money for the title of Shift Accident when he went to relieve himself, threw a lit cigar end in the direction of the toilet pan, and planted his butt upon the butt with excruciating consequences.

All his medical problems revolved around his nether regions; he was taken into hospital for the sort of operation usually performed on males of the Hebrew persuasion at an early age, and returned to work in some discomfort, commenting that "he wasn't much of a surgeon, but he was good at embroidery."

His master-stroke, however, occurred when the English cup final was due to be televised. This coincided with the Scottish final, and BBC Scotland were transmitting the Scottish match in preference.

"I ain't watchin' that crap," said he, "I'm gonna watch the Spurs gime, mite!"

To achieve this feat he purchased a television in London and brought it up to Shetland on the premise that, since it was an English television set, it would receive the English cup final.

His disappointment was profound.

ENGINEERS AND OTHER ANIMALS

During the commissioning of the terminal's gas plant, financial profligacy was rife. One of the weirder purchases was a quantity of condoms. When one considers that males buying three of this product are renowned for last-minute attacks of stage fright, resulting in the purchase of bottles of aspirin, one has to admire the brass neck of the commissioning manager who asked for a gross of them, allegedly to seal open vents on the plant.

This was topped, however, by another member of the commissioning team, who decided to order twenty cupholders for the plastic coffee cups supplied by the coffee machines on site.

Unfortunately his pen had a minor brainstorm while he was filling out the requisition, and instead of twenty cupholders, he got twenty boxes, a total of twenty thousand; there were so many that the company had to buy additional portacabins in which to store them and, to add insult to injury, the vending manufacturer changed the design of the cups, as a result of which the new ones didn't fit the cupholders.

A normal human being would have been embarrassed; the perpetrator of this particular gaffe, however, was an engineer, and we had long ago realised that this species is born with an inbuilt immunity to any form of embarrassment.

Engineers in general were held in the same sort of awe displayed by mediaeval society towards leprosy sufferers, usually with good reason. One specimen went walking on an isolated beach one Sunday afternoon and discovered a device which his years of training led him to assume was an unexploded bomb. A bomb disposal squad appeared a few hours later, less than amused at being dragged from the pub. Their demeanour was not improved when they discovered the suspect explosive device was a redundant Cortina steering wheel.

It took me a long time to figure out the difference between a fitter and an engineer, but it's really fairly straightforward.

A fitter repairs things.

An engineer devises systems to ensure that before the fitter can fix anything somebody has to write out a work order, forty other people have to process it, a computer has to prioritise it, a manager has to authorise it, a clerk has to file it, an accountant has to cost it, and a supervisor has to decide if the job can be fitted into the work schedule.

This is an excellent system. By the time the fitter gets round to doing the job, the equipment is obsolete and the parts are no longer available.

The ladies of commissioning were not averse to the occasional blush. One damsel, rather well endowed in the pectoral area, decided to test out her new bikini in Lerwick swimming pool. All went well until she tried a handstand in the shallow end, as a result of which the forces of gravity took charge of her upper anatomy and her bosoms fell out of her costume. Not to be outdone, her dentures promptly came out in support, and she was faced with an unenviable choice between salvaging her modesty or her dignity.

Gas commissioning in our area was the responsibility of Willy Makem, who was so laid back he was horizontal; his sole interest appeared to be mooning lustfully over page three of a certain alleged newspaper, and the world outside its pages was little more than a minor distraction.

The problems of the plant were of no consequence when compared to those of "Worried, Surbiton", on page seventeen; the world of compressors and chillers was drab indeed when compared with the multitude of sexual problems and deviations of *Sun* readers. Willy's fixation with a nether world of lacy basques and highly imaginative sexual practices caused some disruption to his work schedule; he would frequently turn up at meetings too late, too early – frequently days too early – and events soon proved that his confusion was contagious.

In nominal charge of the personnel department was Ian French, who sported a large beard which was reputedly the home for a family of hooded crows. He was an accomplished musician, and was a virtuoso on the penny whistle.

He also had the happy knack of lapsing into a coma during management-union meetings, and management harangues on the need to cut costs and dispense with dead wood were followed by angry silences from the union side, broken only by the gentle snorings of the representative

"A design engineer, are ye?...never mind, son, when the recession's ower ye can get yersel' a real job..."

of the personnel department.

The department, in the early days at least, managed to spend the company's money with a largesse which would have made the late Captain Bob green with envy. Vast lakes of alcohol were poured down the throats of new recruits in the hope that they could also swallow the recruitment spiel; the main exponent of this philosophy was a character named Mike Hatton, who must have personally dished out in moving-up expenses the company's profits to date. He was an officer in the Royal Naval Reserve, and perceived it as his duty to procure for the crews of visiting warships sufficient eligible young ladies to go around. It was somewhat uncharitably suggested that he had learned this art in the red light district of Hong Kong. His underling was Duncan Brown, known to all as Drunken Duncan. He left the terminal under a cloud shortly after he interviewed a candidate for a jetty operator's job and wrote him a letter telling him that his application for the post of nurse had been successful.

Times changed, however, and a damage limitation exercise took place in personnel. A new man arrived to replace Mike Hatton, who returned to the bowels of Britannic House, which was the company's Imperial Palace in London, and which had allegedly a larger cast of comic singers than the Palladium.

The new man was a Glaswegian, who claimed to come from Kelvinside, where sex is what the coal is delivered in; it was, however, alleged that he really came from Partick – where they drink their Beaujolais straight from the bottle – but suffered delusions of grandeur.

His dress sense was unusual to say the least; he made Beau Brummel look like a railroad bum and smoked a brand of pipe tobacco that smelled like gorilla body odour. He promptly bought himself a large property on the island, and discovered to his glee that along with the house came a title. Within a short time he was styling himself MacDuff of Bargord – which was the name of his house.

The proletariat on site, who regarded self-proclaimed aristocrats with the same deference displayed towards the upper classes by the Paris mob in 1791, promptly bastardised his title to MacDuff of Fireguard.

Shortly after the new laird took up residence in Chateau Bargord, a letter arrived from a former member of the Norwegian resistance. Many Norwegians had come to Shetland during the war, and busied themselves running guns and explosives across the North Sea to enable the stay-at-home Norskis to demonstrate their appreciation of the Wehrmacht in positive terms.

The laird's correspondent claimed to have been one of the aforesaid resistance members, and his letter described how, in expectation of a German invasion, he had buried a large quantity of kroner in the grounds of Chateau Bargord, which had been a major resistance base at the time.

It never occurred to the MacDuff to question why his benefactor should choose to impart such information to a complete stranger, or why he had not dug up the booty in the period since the final whistle in 1945; specific directions were given to enable the treasure to be recovered, and the laird set about excavating the grounds of Bargord with feverish enthusiasm. The only fruits of his labours were a number of small metal cups, which turned out to be the remains of a long-forgotten putting green, but no treasure was unearthed.

It wasn't until he consulted a map of Norway that he discovered that his informant's address was somewhat suspect.

Not even a Norwegian would live in a place called Arsefiord.

Delusions of grandeur were not confined to the personnel department. One of the Ninian inspectors was a former naval officer who regularly returned from shopping trips to the mainland clutching a Harrods shopping bag. Rumour had it that he made his purchases in Oxfam, and put them in a carrier bag looted from Harrod's bin.

One day he turned up with a cat, reputedly purchased from the Top Store. It was no ordinary moggie, being a Burmese Blue, and had a better pedigree than the Queen. Two days after he bought it his wife reversed the car over it. He was most dischuffed when Harrods refused to replace it under guarantee.

THE BERRS

During this period construction of the terminal was in full flood, and the construction workforce were accommodated in two huge camps near the Firth and Mossbank estates, with more being housed in two redundant ferries adjacent to the terminal.

The camps provided a focal point for many local residents, and also jobs for some of the wives. One group of the latter spent much of their free time socialising in the camp bars, and the fact that they were not Kim Bassinger lookalikes was reflected in their collective title of the Doris Karloffs.

The Scottish tabloid press took a keen interest in the camps, populated as they were by thousands of bachelors far from home. These the press dubbed 'Rugged Oil Bears'. Since most of the construction workforce were, by and large, small and scrawny, it was hardly an apt description.

The amount of money raised among the construction workers for charity over the years was unbelievable, as was the variety and standard of acts brought up from south by the social committees to entertain them. It was reasonable to assume that, with so much cash flying about, there would be rumours of financial chicanery, and one such rumour reached a Sunday paper, which sent an ace reporter up to ferret out a story.

The next week the paper ran a centre page spread about a Viking ghost called Lek who was terrorising the Rugged Oil Bears of "Crazy K" Block, which, as it turned out, was built on the site of an ancient Norse rubbish dump.

It made much more interesting reading than alleged fiddling at bingo, and proved conclusively that investigative reporters are just as gullible as personnel officers.

One berr from the emerald isle made enquiries about how he might transport a Shetland pony to the mainland, and was told he could probably do it by boat, and that he should make arrangements through the local RSPCA. "I can't do that..." said he, "...I'm not buyin' the powny, I'm stealin' it..."

One clan which worked on the terminal were the Kerr family from Glasgow, which consisted of Daddy Kerr and his four sons, known

"...as I was saying to my manicurist the other day, being a rugged oil bear is murder on my fingernails...and as for the effect on one's coiffure of these blasted hard hats..."

collectively as the Kerr Berrs or, less flatteringly, the Four Kerrs. When three of them went on leave they always left the Wan Kerr behind.

OPENING TIME

Towards the end of 1980 someone in Britannic House noticed Sullom Voe on a map, and decided that it was time it was officially opened. Feelers were put out for a person of suitable eminence to perform the ceremony, but Mickey Mouse was busy and Ronald Biggs had a slight problem with his passport, so the Corporate Empire was in a quandary.

Fortunately the Queen fancied a few days off and the *Britannia* and a naval frigate were sitting around doing nothing, so she said she and the Chooky Embra would take a wee turn up after the new year to open the place.

Needless to say, the impending royal visit caused a massive flurry of activity, and the company dipped deeply into its post office account in an effort to make the site look pretty. One of the major problems was an area adjacent to the terminal gates which contained an apparatus euphemistically known as a clargester, which was in fact the terminal sewage treatment plant.

The plant was all below ground level, the only indication of its presence being the ozone layer which hung about the area like a cloud of nerve gas, and had the fortunate side effect of concealing the cooking smells from the nearby kitchens.

It was decided, however, that the presence of the clargester might offend Her Majesty's eyes, and a large and very impressive timber wall was built around it.

When dawn broke on the morning of the visit, it became obvious to Her Majesty's loyal minions on the terminal that disaffected republican elements had been at work overnight.

Emblazoned in ten foot high letters on the clargester wall was the legend "FORT TURD".

Shortly after that there was a seamen's strike, as a result of which there was no freight from the British mainland. The islands soon ran out of basics such as vegetables and bread, and one entrepreneur decided that, in view of the shortages, it might be a good idea to take a boat down to Wick and pick up a few essentials.

He was a large and somewhat intimidating character, and had no difficulty persuading the skipper of a fishing boat to put to sea on such an errand of mercy. His return was greeted with undisguised relief by the patrons of the Royal British Legion, Lerwick, for the vessel was filled to the gunwales with cases of beer.

THE POWER OF THE PRESS

One of the difficulties experienced by shift staff on the terminal was the interference caused to the social whirl by night and weekend work, and it was not uncommon to receive calls in the control room, about an hour before the relieving shift was due to arrive, from individuals suffering from weird and wonderful ailments which would undoubtedly prove both contagious and fatal if they were foolhardy enough to turn up for work. Ailments of this sort tended to reach epidemic proportions around the time of Up Helly Aa (A Shetland festival held in January during which the population dresses up, sets fire to a boat, and then gets drunk), folk festivals, lambing, and yacht regattas.

One unfortunate, off work with terminal diarrhoea, had the misfortune to appear in a photograph on the front page of *The Shetland Times*, lewdly eyeing up a sheep at a livestock sale; another, incapacitated with a slipped disc, appeared in the same publication performing an eightsome reel with hysterical gusto.

DON'T TELL ME YOUR TROUBLES...

Travelling by bus is normally considered pretty stress free and relaxing; not, however, in the case of one maintenance contractor who had overdosed on Guinness and vindaloo the night before.

Five minutes after the commencement of his journey to work, he asked the bus driver to stop the bus in order that he might relieve himself at the side of the road.

"Jist hang on, till we get tae work, pal," said the driver, conscious of the fact that he was driving an express bus.

A few minutes later his passenger was back, white-faced and entreating him again through clenched teeth to stop the bus.

"Cannae dae that," said the driver impatiently. "Ah've goat a schedule tae meet."

On the third occasion the contractor warned him somewhat forcibly that if he did not get off pretty fast the bus was going to be visited by a rather unpleasant accident.

The driver pulled over to the side of the road and the passenger leapt out; when the driver noticed him frantically pulling his trousers down he realised the nature of the emergency and immediately took off into the wide blue yonder, leaving his erstwhile passenger squatting at the roadside in full view of passing traffic.

In order to save himself embarrassment, the contractor simply pulled his parka hood over his head, prompting passing motorists to speculate on the identity of the bum at the side of the road.

The story had a postscript. The following week he of the faulty bowels approached his shop steward protesting that the company had erroneously deducted payment of a sub from his wages which had already been deducted the previous week.

"That's no problem," said the steward. "Just show the wages clerk last week's payslip to prove you've already paid it."

"Ah cannae dae that!" said the unfortunate complainant, close to tears. "See that time ah wis caught short at the side of the road? Well, therr wis nae leaves or grass aboot an the only bit of paper ah had oan me wis ma payslip!"

THE NAKED TRUTH

The Ninian inspectors, whose alleged role it was to monitor the Ninian pipeline system, were not considered overworked, even by terminal standards. There was, therefore, considerable surprise when their strength was augmented by the appointment of assistant inspectors.

These worthies were carefully selected from among operations personnel on the terminal, and it was cynically held that this was an *en masse* example of promotion by incompetence unrivalled in modern history.

It soon became clear, however, that not all the new appointees had been schooled in corporate diplomacy.

The terminal had a newspaper whose chief – and only – reporter spent a couple of days each month racing around the terminal like a rabid ferret, attempting to find interesting snippets of information with which to fill its pages.

Since company policy prohibited reporting on wife swapping, bestiality with the sheep population and the sort of human interest stories which people really want to read about, the unfortunate hack was frequently reduced to dredging the depths of his imagination to drum up a story.

One day he had a flash of inspiration and decided to run a real exclusive; he was going to spill the beans on the Ninian inspectors and tell the world just what they did to earn their crust.

So it was that he turned up one day in the control room, notepad at the ready and camera at the short trail.

The inspector on duty was blessed with a silver tongue and a remarkably vivid imagination, and spent twenty minutes explaining that his role was beyond the capacity of mere mortals and demanded massive commitment, intellligence and physical stamina.

Having completed his interview with this paragon of industry, the reporter turned to his newly appointed assistant, who was a refugee from Maryhill, an area of Glasgow so dilapidated that its residents daily curse the Germans for missing them out in the Blitz.

"And what do you do?" queried the scribe.

"Well," said the assistant, lolling nonchalantly back in his chair, "He does f... all, and I help him."

For reasons best known to himself, the reporter produced an abridged copy of the interview for publication.

THE DEFENCE OF THE REALM

Following the Falklands war there was a rush to the colours from the non-pacifist elements of staff.

The government in its wisdom had decided to reform the Home Guard under a new title of Local Defence Force, and a recruitment campaign was mounted among the terminal's geriatrics for suitable blood-crazed homicidal maniacs to defend the shores of Shetland from the Red Menace.

The whole scheme was taken remarkably seriously by people who really should have known better. The Ministry of Defence, as usual, excelled itself with its publicity campaign.

This featured two heavily armed and camouflaged soldiers coming over a rise and was captioned:

"One of these soldiers is a regular and one is a territorial; if you were the enemy, would you know the difference?"

It obviously did not occur to the MOD's publicity department that Ivan from Minsk had never heard of the territorial army, and would probably shoot both of them.

The campaign to defend our shores with barricades of heroically dead pensioners fizzled out somewhat, but one individual was so impressed by the ministry's propaganda that he joined the territorials.

He began coming to work in a uniform of camouflage jacket, headband, and three day's growth of beard, presumably to convince his civilian comrades of his status as a weekend Rambo.

His new image was received with some cynicism by his fellows, who easily penetrated his militaristic veneer and saw the six-stone weakling beneath.

In an effort to prove his manhood, the weekend warrior strolled into the control room one evening, placed a stapler against his forehead, and fired it.

He wasn't completely stupid, for he had taken the precaution of unloading it first. Unfortunately for him, he had neglected the first rule of firearms handling – there was still one up the spout, and as a result of his demonstration of machismo his foreheadskin was stapled firmly to the front of his skull. He was saved the embarrassment of a trip to the medical centre when the shift fitter volunteered to remove the staple with a tyre lever.

The power station was a little world apart from the rest of the terminal, and was in a constant state of ferment. All of its senior staff were allegedly born out of wedlock, and not a few, if the masses were to be believed, were the result of an unnatural liaison between a lady of easy virtue and a goat.

There certainly seemed to be an impression that supervisory staff in the area rented their brain cell from the company and put it in their lockers before they went home.

This was illustrated when a member of the supervisory elite decided to invest in a new car, and informed his poverty stricken minions that he planned to buy a top of the range Vauxhall Senator estate.

It came as some surprise, therefore, when he turned up at work a few days later with a Nova estate, which is about the size of a hamster cage with wheels.

His shift were naturally curious about his change of mind; he pointed out that this was indeed a master stroke on his part which had saved him about ten grand, since the Nova and the Senator each had the same amount of luggage space, and the Nova was half the price.

This wisdom was received with some incredulity, since the difference in size between the two cars was substantial.

"I'll prove it to you!" said the elitist, "I'll bring in the brochures!"

Sure enough, there it was in black and white; both cars had the same amount of luggage space.

There was, however, a little asterisk beside this information on the Nova; on the bottom of the page was a significant addendum...'this amount of space can only be achieved by folding the rear seats down...'

THE LODGERS

I spent a long time consigned to the effluent plant, which was widely regarded as the terminal's answer to Devil's Island. It was conceived to extract oil from contaminated ballast water and to handle oil dumped from other areas in the event of a crisis. Megabucks were spent developing

"Fancy a quick jaunt down to the canteen skip to see if there's any cordon bleu on today?"

it, and it was strongly rumoured that the design team had been hired *en masse* from Lada.

Its eccentric behaviour unquestionably represented a challenge to an engineer of the highest calibre. Unfortunately, few of our engineers matched such a description; it was widely held that to qualify as an engineer at Sullom Voe one had to be so incompetent mechanically that promotion to an office was unavoidable in the interests of public safety.

From the day of its first commissioning the effluent plant was awash with a multitude of engineers and boffins, all intent on rectifying the blunders made by the engineers and boffins who had designed it in the first place; all manner of strange plots were hatched to resolve its problems, and as each new plot was put into operation, the plant degenerated into greater depths of mechanical unpredictability.

It was not a fun spot – it was appropriately known to those fated to work in it as the Shitpits – but it had the advantage of being out of the way; as a result the control room was well stocked with crossword books and a quantity of highly questionable literature which was certainly not provided by the Gideon Society.

One night-shift I had given up wrestling with this infernal doomsday machine, and was taxing my cerebral area with a particularly interesting sexual diversion in the pages of *Forum* magazine when the telephone rang.

In the effluent plant the ringing of a telephone equated to a death knell; as a rule it meant that someone somewhere had blundered, and the results of the blunder were heading in one's direction at a rate of knots.

I was surprised on lifting the phone to find that it was dead, so shrugged my shoulders and went for dinner. I had my usual salmonella salad and, on returning to the control room, found a cardboard box sitting on the desk. On opening it, I was somewhat taken aback when a large and somewhat irate crow flew out, circled the control room a couple of times, and landed on a ledge just below the roof.

Needless to say, this development caused me some puzzlement, and I spent some time considering the identity of the person who had delivered it, until I concluded that the rest of the evening might be more profitably spent struggling with the fiendish intricacies of the *Sun* coffee-time crossword.

As it turned out, the crossword drawer was inhabited by yet another crow, who flew up to join his mate. Two hours later I found a third one, which had taken up temporary residence in the dustbin.

During the night my visitors spent their time eying me beadily and giving occasional caws to break the monotony, but come daybreak they arose from their torpor and took to hurtling about the control room like demented Stukas.

At shift change I beat a hasty retreat and handed the job over to my relief; since I did not want to alarm him I omitted to mention the presence of my feathered friends, and he spent an interesting half hour evicting them from the premises with a yard broom.

135

HAPPINESS IS AN ARTEX BATH

8th May 1981, is etched forever in my memory, since it was the day the cat chose to produce a litter of kittens. It was also the day the wife decided to take off for pastures new, but this was lost on me at the time, since the taxi arrived just as the fourth kitten was appearing, and that was more than enough excitement to be going on with.

For some time afterwards I took up residence in the seamen's mission, quaffing large quantities of ale to celebrate my escape from the shackles of marriage; as a result the house became somewhat more neglected than it had been under my erstwhile partner's care. It has to be said that she was herself no devotee of housework; four months after she left I discovered that the net curtains in the bathroom were actually cobwebs.

I decided it was time to start afresh, and concluded that some decorating would be in order. During a moment of madness I was persuaded by a neighbour that my best plan was to have the front room artexed, and that he was the very man to do the job. It was arranged that he would turn up the following Saturday and transform my front room into a showpiece of palatial splendour with this miraculous solution.

He did indeed turn up on the appointed day, which was the only thing that went right. He was a devout inebriate and had been worshipping all morning; as a result his faculties, never exactly strung together at the best of times, were in serious disarray.

His assurance that he could "do this standing on my head" was less than comforting, since he was obviously having considerable difficulty standing on his feet. He spent ten minutes trying to get the drum of artex open; I did not want to offend his artistic sensitivity by pointing out that the reason he couldn't get the lid off was because the drum was upside down.

Eventually he made a start, but after a couple of minutes tactfully suggested that a wee tincture of the water of life wouldn't go amiss. His idea of a tincture, unfortunately, was the contents of the bottle, and this had a rather detrimental effect on his technique with the roller.

After twenty minutes I managed to persuade him that, having watched his masterly performance, I thought I had grasped enough to finish the job, and suggested that he should perhaps go home and gird his loins for another session in the mission that evening.

The front room looked like the result of an explosion in a Christmas grotto; there was white artex everywhere with the exception of the walls, which was where it was supposed to be. After that I stopped having delusions about having my abode featured in *Home and Garden* and decided I could learn to live in a state of hoveldom.

A DEATH IN THE FAMILY

I decided I would keep one of the cat's offspring, which I named Microbe because it looked like one. The dog, being a qualified escapologist, soon trained the felines to open windows, and I frequently got halfway to the bus stop for work only to discover that I was being trailed by a herd of escaped domestic pets.

On one occasion the mother cat, which was a remarkably objectionable white animal, followed me up the road to the bus stop, and ignored my orders to her to return home. I went on past the stop to post a letter, and was picked up by a workmate in his car.

A few seconds later we came upon the body of the white cat at the roadside; a quick check proved that she had gone through the Great Catflap in the Sky.

I spent the night-shift being assailed through the site radios with plaintive miaows from my sympathetic workmates, and went home the following morning, got a black bag, put the corpse in it, and started digging a hole in the garden. "Garden" was a misnomer; the only things that grew in it were rocks, and it took twenty minutes to dig a hole big enough for the dearly departed.

I backfilled the hole, and made a short eulogy to the effect that "That's the last time you'll shit on the front room carpet, pal!" I left the graveside and walked into the kitchen to find the cat eyeing me with its usual malicious sneer.

I don't know whose cat I buried that day, but it wasn't mine.

PROMOTIONS

The way to the stars in the corporate galaxy was a tortuous route indeed. The logic governing promotions was totally incomprehensible and was the subject of much speculation, especially among those who lusted after higher things but fell with monotonous regularity at the first fence. There was little question that some of those whom the company selected to climb the metaphorical ladder were incapable of the sort of rational thought which would enable them to get past the first rung on a real ladder.

The routes to the top were manifold; there was a widely held belief at one point that, since the upper echelons tended to play golf rather than pool or darts, then one's promotion chances would be dramatically increased by taking up the sport of kings. The failure of this particular strategy became evident when the notice boards around the terminal blossomed with advertisements for expensive sets of golf bats, little used, and cheap for quick sale.

Some people – few and far between, it has to be said – got there through sheer talent, but the most common philosophy seemed to be grovelling, and the adherents of this particular method could be readily identified by the burnt sienna hue of their nasal apparatus. The classic success story in this respect was the character who called both his children after the operations manager, and openly boasted that he had voted for Maggie Thatcher. The fact that he was good at his job was irrelevant.

The most popular promotion in offsites was that of a certain shift controller, whose elevation out of the area to take charge of the fire department was the cause of much joy among his former subjects. Brian Edison's move, however, was less than enthusiastically received by his new minions, who considered that their new chief was somewhat lacking in the milk of human kindness. Their opinion was soon revised downwards, and he was rapidly re-assessed as Satan Incarnate.

This view of his talents worried the new boss not one whit, and he positively revelled in the contention that he was Old Nick's ambassador on earth, considering that his minions were all devotees of solo sexual

THE PROMOTION INTERVIEWEE LEARNS ABOUT DELEGATION OF RESPONSIBILITY

"Imagine the scenario...the tanker on jetty three is on fire...there's a major gas leak in process and a terminal wide power failure...given these circumstances, who would you blame?"

malpractices.

He was an avid and somewhat vigorous football player, and his numerous sendings-off for committing GBH on his opponents were greeted with unashamed glee among his troops. He had, however, mastered the art of morale control, and kept those below him in a constant state of false hope by putting it about that his transfer elsewhere was imminent, and ensuring that the transfer, for which his troops prayed to every god in the celestial firmament, never actually materialised.

He attended meetings with the union as his department's management representative, and as such was very popular with his fellow managers, who could sit back happy in the knowledge that if there was any flak flying about it was certain to be going in Brian's direction.

His grasp of English was somewhat sparse; when he was accused of being "economical with the truth" during one meeting he sat in silent contemplation for about an hour before suddenly storming out of the room shouting that he wasn't staying to be insulted.

FAMINE IN THE LAND

There was considerable change at the top of the tree during the first few years; the senior managers who had assured the lower classes, hand on heart *à la* Ronald Reagan, that Shetland was a job for life and that they were totally committed to the archipelago, had a tendency to cut and run with bewildering frequency. Tom Harkins vapourised in the middle of a telephone call. His replacement had a short stay on the terminal, and seemed to spend most of it playing golf and beating all comers, it being considered hazardous to one's career to beat the boss.

The third manager was an entirely different version of Corporate Man. Claude Dillinger bore a startling resemblance to Sergeant Bilko, and soon made it obvious that he subscribed wholeheartedly to the Hangem Floggem School of Industrial Relations.

From day one our conditions were, by and large, far ahead of normal industry standards. Meals were free, and each morning and evening filled rolls and other goodies were delivered to the messrooms on site.

The first indication of impending change came when the peanuts disappeared from the delivery; this caused some disquiet, especially in the power station, where most of the shift oran-utang population were housed.

Shortly after that the new manager deemed that rolls were a luxury which the company could ill afford, since the price of crude had plummeted to forty dollars a barrel and there was a need for drastic economies. It was rumoured that the company chairman had stopped dining at the Reform Club and was subsisting on steak and kidney pie in the saloon of the Ruptured Duck.

Claude duly stopped the rolls and full-scale revolt broke out; the lower echelons were baying for blood and the manager was in severe danger of becoming an involuntary donor. The Sergeant Bilko image dissolved, to be replaced by one of an ogre stalking the land and leaving famine in his wake.

In a desperate attempt to curry favour, Claude used the favourite ploy of dictators to hold his crumbling empire together and started a purge of the Taffia, as the Welsh management cabal were known.

The Taffia had become about as popular as a cardinal in an Orange lodge, primarily because they seemed to spend most of their time flying down to Britain to watch their alleged rugby team being put through the mincer, and the rest of the time reminiscing about the Land of Their Fathers.

It was the general consensus of opinion on the terminal that there wasn't a Welshman on the planet who knew who his father was. It was therefore extremely good thinking on Claude's part to target the Taffia for extermination, and he set about it with ruthless efficiency.

Welshmen were soon disappearing like snow off a dyke. The hapless industrial relations officer found himself boxed up and exiled to Dyce; he was replaced by a Shetlander who turned out to be a latent socialist and had a very short stay indeed. The emergency services superintendent went offshore, a career move which was certainly traumatic; he was alleged to be the only man in the North Sea to suffer from pre-menstrual tension. The operations manager, who was hoping to end his days in a quiet little pumping station in the Aberdeenshire Oilie Belt, found himself shunted off to the Peoples' Republic of China, a career move which was widely considered by those he left behind as a just reward for services rendered.

The year Claude arrived the annual Saint David's Day dinner was held in Lerwick Town Hall; the next one was held in a telephone kiosk and was attended by the sole surviving Taff and his girlfriend. The latter did not enjoy the occasion and bleated all the way home.

As the man said: 'The evil that men do lives after them, the good is oft interred with their bones.' Nobody in Sullom Voe remembers how Claude disposed of the Taffia, but he'll go down in history as the man who stopped the rolls.

THE RATTLE OF MUSKETRY

At about the same time we got a new foreman and shift controller. The foreman was a Shetlander, an amiable chap who was really far too nice for the job (or for the company, for that matter).

He was far too trusting for his own good, a situation which was exploited to the full by his shift. As a result of a message left on his desk he became the four hundred and thirty-second person to phone Glasgow Zoo on 1 April 1987, who was returning a call from Mr C. Lyon.

His main problem was that he took the job seriously; most of us had long realised that such an approach produced only chronic ulcers and entries in the obituary columns of the company newspaper.

He exuded an image of professional competence which was severely dented when someone came across some pictures of him in a ballet dress taken during an Up Helly Aa celebration. Rumour had it that following terminal-wide circulation of this material, he was taken quietly to one side and told that if he ever took his trousers off in front of a camera again he'd be sacked.

The shift controller, Johnny Sim, was a different animal. He bore a startling resemblance to Claude, and seldom left his office during the night-shifts, lest he be assassinated by mistake.

Johnny Sim was the only man I ever met who could split an expletive with another expletive; his command of Anglo-Saxon was incredible. He was a former miner, the coal board's gain being our loss. He had also spent some time as an RAF driver in the Middle East during his national service, and seemed to have spent most of it fighting Arabs; in this he was remarkably successful, mainly because the Arabs weren't aware there was a war on, and by the time Aircraftsman Sim's truck hit them it was too late to find out.

Ten minutes of ex-Aircraftsman Sim's reminiscences provided a profound insight into the reasons for the disappearance of the huge lumps of pink bits which once indicated the Imperial Presence on the map of the world.

The shift controller met his nemesis the night the process flare went out. The igniter system was out of commission and the only way to relight the flare was to turn the gas on and fire a shotgun at it (I kid you not). This was no easy feat, since the flare tip was at the top of a tower the height of a high rise flat.

It took some time to broach the news to Johnny; since he was noted for having a somewhat short fuse it was first necessary to find someone brave or stupid enough to tell him. There was some debate over whether

"So far he's wiped out most of the Plough, the Pole Star, and a Russian satellite..."

it might be appropriate to form an impromptu choir and sing the news over the radio, but eventually the youngest member of the shift was volunteered to carry out the job.

Controller Sim's cerebral matter went into critical mass, and his brain cells were popping like Rice Krispies; he was not a happy man. After five minutes of obscene fulminations, he broke out the shift shotgun and set off to the flare.

He was followed, at a safe distance, by a large retinue of would-be spectators, who had never seen the flare being lit with a shotgun before.

They were to be disappointed.

Their intrepid leader blazed away for hours at the flare, and the rattle of musketry echoed around the landscape; so dire was his shooting that even the rabbits came out to watch. Eventually, suffering from battle fatigue, he passed his thunder stick to the control room operator, who lit the flare with his first shot.

His mood was not improved when someone rather undiplomatically suggested that if they'd pinned a picture of Yasser Arafat on the flare tip he'd have hit it first time.

RUST

One day a Rugged Oil Bear was stripping away insulation when he noticed some brown stuff on the pipework. Within hours the plant was awash with boffins and engineers who pronounced that the terminal was infested with rust. This caused some furore; Rolls Royce oil terminals are not supposed to rust, far less suffer terminal decay, and it had the potential to greatly embarrass the Empire. It was decided, therefore, that what had been discovered was really CUI, which meant Corrosion Under Insulation and which was, of course, something much more in keeping with the terminal's image.

The local newspaper hacks, however, were well acquainted with the company's obsession with euphemisms; for instance they knew that when a company spokesman said that the plant was experiencing minor technical problems, it was a pretty safe bet that the difficulties were of sufficient magnitude to produce a lot of involuntary bowel movement among those whose job it was to put things back on an even keel.

Within hours the vultures were circling around the door of the hapless public relations officer. This worthy was a former wing commander in the air force; he did not broadcast the fact, however, that his wing consisted of Chipmunk trainers, which are about as hi-tech as a coal-fired microwave, and have the airborne agility of a legless platypus.

The squadron leader's speciality was performing a variety of highly suggestive songs when in his cups, and he spent his waking moments – which were few and far between – trekking around the uninhabited parts of Shetland, and writing books about his travels. It had never occurred to him that the uninhabited parts of Shetland were devoid of humanity because everyone else had long since decided that they weren't worth inhabiting anyway.

The squadron leader, faced with legions of baying pressmen with the scent of an Armageddon story, reacted with his customary aplomb, and blurted out that rust wasn't unusual, and that even his Volkswagen was rusty.

The significance of this was somewhat lost in translation, for the connection between his car and an oil terminal was somewhat obscure, to say the least, and it was felt that perhaps this was not exactly a stunning example of how best to head off a public relations crisis.

Shortly afterwards a letter, allegedly from the squadron leader to the Chairman of Volkswagen appeared on noticeboards around the site. It read:

Mein Herr,

Das autowagen Volks ich haf purchasen. Das steelwerken ist kaput. Himmel! das kat ist spitten through it. Das autowagen ist nicht worth ein scheissen, ist as gut as ein gefahrt in ein klappersturm.

Das doors ist gefallen offen, das ventilatten in das winter ist chillenoffen das goebbels. Ich bein ein Grossnfuhrer mit der grosse englischer petroleum. Mein wagen must be gut, nicht der Deutche krappen I haf.

Night wonder du losen der krieig das Kruat schweinhund. Next time ich purchasen ein Englischer autowagen. Ich purchasen ein Nissan.

Sticken der Volkswagen uppen das Poffenpassagen.

yours sincerely...

THE BOAT PEOPLE

The population of Mossbank changed dramatically as time passed; the council houses emptied of oilies, who either bought their own property or moved into company houses, and new residents seldom remained for any length of time.

There was a growing perception that the area, which certainly held little appeal for native Shetlanders, was becoming a prime site for housing what the quality press calls "socially deprived elements"; this suspicion was heightened when a run-down caravan site was closed and a large percentage of its residents were housed in the area.

This situation arose at about the same time as people were leaving the Socialist Utopia of Vietnam in droves, and the new Mossbank arrivals were quickly dubbed the Hillswick Boat People.

They seemed to infest the main roads of the area, and used one hand for thumbing lifts and the other for clutching cans of export.

I was walking the dog one evening when one of them hailed me from a distance. I feigned deafness, but he ran after me.

"Haw Jimmy," said he, betraying his mainland origins, "Wid ye mind giein' me a haun' tae move a fridge up tae ma hoose?"

I agreed to help him, and spent the next hour or so assisting my new acquaintance – whom I shall call Jimmy – to transfer his burden. Our progress was somewhat impeded since he could only use one hand for the fridge, the other being laden with a gigantic kerryoot from which he partook liberally *en route*.

Next morning I went to work and was in the messroom when one of my fellow workers came in.

"Nothing's sacred around Mossbank any more," he stormed. "Some thieving git stole a fridge from outside my door last night!"

His anger was only exceeded by my embarrassment.

One evening a resident was sitting in his front room supping a wee libation when Jimmy came through the door.

This surprised him somewhat, since he knew Jimmy only by reputation, and that was enough to cause him to hide his remaining libation with some dispatch.

Jimmy plonked himself down on the settee and fixed the resident with a bleary eye.

"Zat yir motor ootside?" inquired Jimmy.

The resident assumed that he had left his lights on and that Jimmy had come in to tell him.

"Aye," said he, "it is...why?"

"Ony chance ye could gie me a run tae Voe?" said Jimmy. "The polis is after me."

The resident advised him somewhat curtly to make his way into the middle distance in short, sexually orientated jumps.

Jimmy soon became a fixture in the ditches of the parish, and eventually petitioned the council for a new house, giving as his grounds for a transfer that "Ah canny stay sober in Mossbank."

JINGLE BELLS

The postal service in Shetland was a pretty hit and miss affair; it was often the case that the bulk of the mail ended up being collected by its intended recipients from the Mossbank pub, and the area went through numerous postpeople during my time in residence. One prime specimen was called Postman Pat. His name wasn't Pat, and he certainly wasn't on the Royal Mail's list for the Christmas honours. Christmas, in fact, was very nearly his undoing; he forsook his uniform on Christmas Eve and started his round in a Santa Claus suit. His customers, unfortunately, were impressed with his initiative in entering the festive spirit, and pressed upon him large quantities of the sort of spirit which would have had a detrimental effect on his senses had he been blessed with any in the first place.

There was at that time an estate called Upper Lea, which was composed of what the company euphemistically called chalet bungalows. They were, in fact, wooden huts, and bore a remarkable similarity to the choice real estate featured in films such as *The Great Escape* and *The Bridge over the River Kwai*. It was in this estate that Postman Pat made his last call on Christmas Eve.

The children had just returned from school, and one of them was told that she should go to a neighbour's house and pick up a Christmas present.

Off she went into the night, to return a few minutes later crying her heart out.

After she had calmed down her mother elicited from her that the reason for her distress was that Santa was dead. "Don't be silly," said the fond parent, "Of course he isn't!"

"But he *IS!*" wailed the child, "I've seen his body!"

And so it came to pass that the mother and child didst go forth into the night, and lo, a few leagues away they didst come upon in a ditch, the body of Postman Pat clad in the garments of Santa.

Postman Pat duly recovered, and spent the next few days rehearsing his New Year's Eve role of Superman; this plot was scotched when he received a somewhat stiff note from his superiors pointing out that delivering Her Majesty's mail in blue tights and red Y-fronts would be viewed as a dismissable offence.

His master stroke, however was pulled when his mother-in-law and her sister came up for a summer break in Shetland.

The Seamens' Mission had an annual Midsummer Eve barbecue which was a major event in the social calendar; as a rule the evening was blessed with traditional Shetland summer weather of hurricane force winds which put the building as well as the sausages at risk, especially as the cooking was usually done by inebriates from the terminal fire department.

On this particular occasion, however, the weather was positively Hawaian, and most of the celebrants turned up in dress appropriate for a balmy summer's evening.

Not Postman Pat's relatives, however.

Having been persuaded by the miscreant that it was a fancy dress do, they had spent a week preparing for the occasion, and turned up clad from head to toe in furry rabbit suits.

ENLIGHTENING THE MASSES

Claude was replaced by a Scotsman from the island of Bute, and his major impact on the terminal was the introduction of a much vaunted safety system.

This was based on cost analysis; if for instance, a compressor blew up, it might cost the company a couple of million. If an operator happened to be playing with it at the time and became terminally dismantled in the process, then a further few quid might have to be claimed from the insurance.

The scheme also involved a major evaluation of operating practices which was called job task analysis. It will be readily apparent to anyone who has read this far that such a scheme could only be dreamed up by an American.

It appeared to operate on the sound premise that the scheme is so complex and time consuming that the workforce are far too busy trying to unravel its complexities to find time for work, never mind accidents.

It was unmatched as a job creation programme; hordes of people whose role in the scheme of things had previously been shrouded in mystery suddenly found themselves in key positions in the new hierarchy.

Vast sums were spent converting cynical heathens to salvation via the programme; the company sent out missionaries into the furthest corners of the Sullom colony preaching the Word.

Seminars were organised and little cards placed on the tables exhorting the participants to smile and get involved in the spirit of this new enlightenment.

Eventually, to the accompaniment of much fanfare from a company propaganda machine which would have made the late Joe Goebbels, MD, green with envy, Sullom Voe achieved the star rating to which it had aspired.

A framed diploma was hung in the canteen with considerable ceremony in order that the tribespeople could share in the sense of achievement.

Two days later somebody stole it.

THE MARINERS

The jetty area had a large number of neanderthals, who lurched around the waterfront, their knuckles dragging along the ground, grunting incomprehensibly.

To stop them getting in the way, the company gave them radios and called them jetty supervisors.

They were all allegedly master mariners, although it was difficult to establish in whose merchant marine they had achieved this distinction; it was widely believed that they had become certificated by collecting the requisite number of coupons for a *Sun* special offer.

Our first foreman docker had an attack of sound common-sense and disappeared back to sea after a couple of months, to be replaced by a character who bore with some fortitude the surname Batt; in a perverse attempt at wit he named his house the Belfry. One day while a neighbour was walking his dog he was accosted by a passing motorist who asked him where the Batts lived.

"In the Belfry," answered the neighbour, and was somewhat taken aback when the motorist snarled, "Funny ha ha, you smart ****!" and drove off in a tantrum.

Batt had a short innings, and was followed by a Geordie who sounded as if he spoke English in reverse. His radio transmissions lasted about a fortnight, were liberally sprinkled with "wey ayes" and other meaningful phrases,and his batteries were usually flat before he had completed the first sentence.

As part of his duties he went on to tankers with paperwork for the master. During the course of one such expedition he was called on the

radio and asked his location

"Eeeeehhh," said he, "Wey aye, I'm down on the ship and I'm looking for the bridge...eeehhhh..."

As his radio clicked off an anonymous voice came over the airwaves: "You can't miss it.....it's the big box at the blunt end of the boat..."

He had an unfortunate knack of taking things at face value, being a somewhat trusting soul, and this came to light when the company, in a totally uncharacteristic display of concern for the workers' welfare, decided to replace the former Soweto shack, which had served as a base for the marine squad, with a real hut.

While this edifice was under construction, Wey Aye decided to check on progress, and in the course of his tour wandered into the room which was to serve as the office for the jetty supervisors, or tanker wardens as

"She's comin' in a wee bit fast, Magnie...jist fend her off wi' the boathook as she comes alongside..."

they were more accurately known. This room was acting, for the duration of construction, as a base for the brickie's card school, which was in full flood when our hero walked in.

He surveyed the room, and his countenance took on a concerned look.

"Eeeehhhhhh," said he, slowly. (His sentences always opened with this sound; we never did find out what it meant.) "Where's the window?"

The workers looked at him blankly for a moment, and the dealer, a large Glasgow gent who obviously used his forehead as a rivet gun, asked "Windae? Thurr's nae windae in here, Jimmy!"

"Wey aye," expostulated Wey Aye. "There's got to be a window! How am ah supposed tae watch the boaats gangin' oot an' in if ah divny have a window? Wey aye, ye'll need tae put in a window!"

The building was duly completed, and sure enough, a window on the world was provided for the foremen dockers.

A few days after completion a letter from the company arrived in Wey Aye's mail tray.

It pointed out that there was no provision in the building's plans for a window, the fitting of which had resulted in considerable additional expense. There followed an itemised account of the costs involved, with the demand that, since Wey Aye had authorised the work, he would be expected to foot the bill.

Within seconds of receiving this missive, Wey Aye was on the telephone to the shift controller, who gave him a sympathetic ear as he fulminated about the injustice being visited upon him by the Gods.

"Who sent the letter?" asked the shift controller.

"It's from the construction and roads department and it's signed T.A.R. Macadam," wailed Wey Aye. "Bloody stupid name if you ask me..."

There was a thunderous crash as a multitude of pennies dropped simultaneously, and it dawned on Wey Aye that he had been severely had.

The marine contingent had within its ranks a number of individuals who were widely suspected of being somewhat left of centre in their sexual leanings; this manifested itself when a youthful graduate engineer was attached to the jetty area to get a taste of sea air.

News of his imminent arrival reached the jetty messroom, and hasty preparations were made to provide a suitable seafarers' welcome.

When the starry-eyed youth came into the messroom to introduce himself, he was confronted by the sight of the shift enthusiastically applauding the efforts of two large sailors in a compromising position on the dinner table.

His stay on the jetties was very brief indeed.

As part of her duties my then current wife boarded visiting tankers to have the master sign cargo documentation.

On visiting one vessel in the early hours of the morning, she was somewhat surprised to find a reception committee of grinning Filipinos awaiting her on the deck. It soon became obvious to her that their intentions were less than honourable, as they followed her to the bridge passing comments on her anatomy, making comments in Filipino roughly equating to "Will ye look at the size of that erse..."

When she left the ship an hour later the crew were again mustered at the gangway, voicing their disapproval at her departure. It was only when she went into the jetty building that she discovered that she'd been sold to the crew by the jetty leading hand.

Speaking from experience, they should count themselves lucky that the deal fell through.

THE HUB OF THE EMPIRE

By the end of the eighties things were getting decidedly sticky; there had been a lot of promotions, and guys who knew what they were doing were becoming thin on the ground.

I did not fit into this category, and there was a strong risk that people like myself, who had lurched along in blissful ignorance for the previous ten years, might actually be expected to play a critical role in the running of the plant, a prospect fraught with potential catastrophe.

Luckily, a job appeared on the notice board for a training technician, and I applied for it. I had no idea what it entailed and was somewhat nonplussed to discover that the personnel superintendent didn't know either; since he had invented the job in the first place, this was somewhat disconcerting.

It was, however, hardly surprising. He played a dame in the annual Lerwick pantomime, and was by all accounts extremely good in the role; it must have rubbed off, since as a personnel superintendent his performance was hilarious.

As luck would have it, I got the job, primarily because I was the only person stupid enough to want it.

In the event, it was something of an eye opener. I spent the next two years wandering around the administration block with bits of paper, passing *en route* dozens of other lost souls who had been doing exactly that for decades.

My opening day set the tone for the future; I was detailed to drive a busload of people to the fire training ground, and couldn't for the life of me remember where it was; quite an achievement considering I had passed the place nearly every day for the preceding ten years.

Things went from bad to worse; a major part of the job was to put new starts on the terminal through an induction course; this opened with a brief explanation of what the terminal actually did.

In my case it was very brief indeed, since I wasn't too sure what it did myself.

I mastered the art of fobbing off the occasional smartasses by couching my explanations in broad rapid-fire Glasgwegian, reasoning that they'd be too busy trying to interpret my brand of extreme Jockanese to analyse the fact that it didn't make any sense whatsoever.

The induction had a video in the middle which was nearly as gripping as the test card, and this gave me the opportunity to slope off for a fag, leaving the victims to suffer half-an-hour or so of utter banality.

This routine went to hell in a basket one day when I had only one inductee to process. I left him to watch the video as usual and then got distracted by a tall lissome creature two offices down the corridor.

Two hours later I remembered him, and returned to the induction room to find the victim glassy-eyed and thoroughly brainwashed, having seen the video over and over again.

Most of the courses were run by tutors brought up at great expense from the mainland. A multitude of subjects were covered, but one that sticks in the mind was the kinetic handling course.

Kinetics is basically the science of lifting things without damaging oneself.

The guy the company selected to run the course had a bad back.

It was also the case that sitting in a classroom all day tended to have a less than stimulating effect on the terminal's working classes, who were more used to life in the open air.

As a result, tutors tended to find that their pupils were prone to dropping off into the Land of Nod, especially after a few pints of liquid stimulus in the Seamen's Mission at lunchtime.

Such was the case with one tutor who, having spent six hours extolling to his enraptured audience the art of scaffolding erection, found that one of his erstwhile pupils had slipped quietly off into the fifth dimension.

The gentle rumblings of his snoring soon attracted the attention of the tutor, who asked a fellow pupil to rescuscitate him.

The pupil fixed him with a stony glare and responded:

"*You* put him to sleep...*you* wake him up."

Working with the collar and tie brigade was somewhat disconcerting. Most of my neighbours were hell bent on corporate stardom and spent their time attending seminars and learning new and meaningless corporate phrases which, by the late eighties, were becoming the only means of communication in the Empire.

The company was striving to change its image and had spent megamillions redesigning its logo into a design for the twenty-first century. The logo was introduced on video by a well-known actor, who obviously needed the money desperately enough to put his credibility on the line by rabbitting on for ten minutes about the virtues of this masterpiece of advertising artwork.

To the unsophisticated, the new logo looked suspiciously like the old one with a slight list to starboard.

Professionalism began to rear its ugly head. We acquired a new operations manager, who looked like a product of an SS Aryan clone factory; he also had a thoroughly Teutonic sense of humour and was widely suspected of having spent the previous twenty years holed up in the Paraguayan jungles.

A new terminal manager also appeared, a remarkably affable character by nature. He bore a startling resemblance to the late Alphonse Capone, and soon earned the soubriquet Luigi.

The new company chairman went on satellite television and gave a rousing oration to the spellbound masses on how the company under his stewardship was going to become a lean mean fighting machine and how he was going to radically change the lives of its employees.

When his brand of corporatese was translated into normal English it became readily apparent that the changes to employees' lives were going to result in huge battalions of them transferring to Maggie's army, more commonly known as the dole queue.

Corporatese became a way of life. Personnel departments were transformed overnight into Human Resources Divisions and the world suddenly became a massive bumf factory.

People spent their whole careers producing reports about reports and then analysing them and producing reports about the analysis. There was more movement of paper around the administration block than through the effluent system of New York in a diarrhoea epidemic.

There were, however, problems in attaining corporate perfection; there was a major hiccup in the infrastructure when process management was moved to the office area.

This was part of a new plan to get managers as far away from their workplace as possible, and was widely perceived by the troops as a thoroughly inspired piece of damage limitation.

One of the arrivals from process was an engineer called George Wilkins. A sophisticate he was not. He was almost certainly the last surviving example of Cro Magnon Man, and communicated via a code of unintelligible grunts.

He originated from Paisley, but had spent many years in Kent, where any vestige of the culture which he had brought from his birthplace had been totally erased. He had spent his formative years in the navy, and had left the service somewhat precipitately after a traumatic experience with an elderly steward in the chain locker.

Standards of behaviour in the corridors of power were rather more decorous than those in the real world outside; groping the cleaners, for instance, was a sacking offence. It became obvious at a very early stage that George's image transformation was going to be a protracted process.

A few days after moving into his office, George was beavering away with the racing section when an acquaintance passed his door. George called after him, but his cry went unheeded, so he lumbered to the corridor and called after him. His message, delivered with a roar which would have been the envy of any self-respecting coalman, roughly translated was:

"Ur ye deaf as well as stupid, ya bastard...did ye no' hear me shoutin' on ye..."

Heads popped from doors. There was a stunned silence as the company identikits peered disapprovingly at him who had sullied their world.

His next-door neighbour from the safety department decided a gentle admonition was in order.

"We're not used to that sort of language down here," he chided.

"Ye ******* ur noo!" snarled George, storming back into his office.

FINALE

By the beginning of 1990 things had got pretty hairy. A new personnel superintendent had replaced the pantomime dame and was, biologically at least, a woman. Her role model was obviously the then prime minister, who was also allegedly a member of the gentler sex, but she was somewhat lacking in the sweet and endearing temperament for which her idol was renowned. Her deputy was a rotund character who bore a superficial resemblance to Oliver Hardy and seemed to have a remarkable propensity for breaking his right wrist. Rumour had it that he was a chronic sufferer from Portnoy's Complaint. (And if you don't know what that is you are almost certainly reading this without glasses.)

I realised fairly early in my new career that my job security was somewhat suspect when the Training Department suddenly disappeared overnight and everyone in it became part of Employee Relations.

Everyone except me.

The message was further rammed home when I was asked to fill out a job description; after racking my brains for two days I conceded defeat and wrote nearly a sentence extolling the importance of my post.

After submitting this literary masterpiece I was somewhat put out to discover that the three guys in the next office, who together had even less to do than me, had managed three pages each.

The writing was obviously on the wall. I had nearly five minutes work to do each day and endeavoured to perfect my timing to ensure that my boss came in slap in the middle of it.

In early 1990 I decided that it was only a matter of time before I was found out, and asked for voluntary severance.

My request was accepted with embarrassing alacrity, and I was given three months to run down the engines prior to my departure from the terminal.

My original boss in training, Wally Tinker, had left the terminal shortly after my arrival. This was somewhat fortuitous, for I had once taken him out on a fishing trip, in the course of which he was violently sick at both ends for the duration of the voyage, and he never forgave me for the experience.

He had departed to Grangemouth, and for some time after he had gone we were plagued with calls asking for various bits and pieces to be sent down to him.

The department had a fairly large video library of training films, most of which had been made on the terminal and were about as gripping as watching an egg-timer. Wally frequently requested copies of these, and it was my job to reproduce them in the video editing suite.

A few days before I left, Wally requested copies of a film, which was, coincidentally scripted and directed by himself, and starred an amazing variety of left feet, starboard ears, and out of focus sheep. The fact that it was designed to illustrate the philosophy behind gas testing would be lost on the casual viewer.

I had, as usual, a lot of time on my hands, and decided to devote considerable effort to the production of Wally's video.

I ran it through a couple of times, and came to the conclusion that Stephen Speilberg had little to fear from Wally. The production was not enhanced by Wally's rather limited vocabulary; when he was stuck for a word he simply said "Hingmie".

This resulted in gems like: "When the gas reaches the lower explosive hingmie and mixes with the hingmie a spark will cause an explosion and blow your hingmie to kingdom come..."

It was patently obvious that Wally's production could stand some professional input, and I had to hand a video which would certainly stimulate the viewer's interest.

It starred a young lady rejoicing in the name of Desiree Cousteau, who had more out front than the battlecruiser *Hood,* and spent her time getting into highly compromising, not to mention visually explicit, situations with the cast of the movie, which included a three-legged aardvark and an oversexed parakeet.

I let the gas testing epic run for two or three minutes to ensure any potential audience would be in a near-comatose condition, then slotted in a second of Miss Cousteau doing some very unusual skydiving with a number of well-endowed male friends. I slotted Miss Cousteau's tasty activities at intervals throughout the video, and at the conclusion of the film I simply filled the blank portion with a selection of artistic shots of the damsel displaying her versatility in a wide variety of unlikely positions.

Having completed the masterpiece to my satisfaction, I stuck it in the post.

The next morning the office telephone rang, and sure enough it was the redoubtable Wally, calling to wish me the best of luck on my imminent departure from the Empire. I waited for the punchline, and it wasn't long in coming.

"By the way," quoth Wally, "did you manage to hingmie that video for me?"

I assured him that the video had been well and truly hingmied, was winging its way to him that very minute, and would probably arrive the following day.

"Great," said Wally, "I'm doing a job task analysis workshop and it will be useful in disseminating information."

"Disseminating" it appeared, was a temporary substitute for "higmie".

A workshop is composed of a group of people who live in a world of their own; workshops are set up so that they can spend their lives discussing how they would handle problems if they lived in the same world as everyone else.

Wally's film arrived on time, and at the appropriate point in the proceedings he announced the Grangemouth premier of his video, switched the machine on, and left the room for a crafty drag.

He returned twenty minutes later to discover his audience staring bug-eyed at Miss Cousteau, who was having a close encounter of a highly personal nature with the aardvark.

Wally was flabbergasted and immediately switched the video off, to the extreme displeasure of the workshop personnel, who had just discovered the real world and were most impressed.

A few seconds later the phone rang at Sullom Voe.

"You incompetent clown!" screeched Wally amiably, "You should have checked that tape before you made my recording... there's a blue movie at the end of it."

"Good grief!" said I. "How strange... thanks for the tip, Wally. I'll check the rest of the stock...I hope it didn't cause you any problems..."

"Problems!!!" he shrieked, "Of course it caused me problems! What do you think it's done to my professional reputation!"

I thought it perhaps impolitic to suggest that Wally's professional reputation was already moribund without any help from outside sources; in view of his emotional state, I also thought it better not to suggest that he check the rest of the film; as it was he simply rewound the tape to the conclusion of the gas test recordings and wiped to the end of the tape, totally oblivious to the fact that there were flashes of Miss Cousteau all the way through it.

As a result his workshops soared in popularity and Wally was deluded into thinking that perhaps the pundits were wrong and he really was good at something after all.

It was some time before he found out the truth; by that time I was long gone.

EPILOGUE

And so it came to pass that the scribe didst go forth from the land of Sullom and verily, didst seek pastures new.

And he didst wander long in that wilderness which is called Britain, and he didst seek labour in the vineyards of the land. But alas, a Shetlander, who calleth himself La Mont, didst appoint himself Chief Pharisee in the counting house of the land, and, verily, he maketh a pig's ear of it.

And the legions of the land toileth not, but didst queue in hordes at the jobcentres, rending their garments and wailing: Gie untae us a joab, fur verily we ur scunnert.

And so it came to pass that the scribe reapeth not, neither did he sow, and in the fullness of time the publican in his ale house sayeth unto him: Render unto me the shekels that thou owest, for verily thy slate is full and runneth over.

And he didst trek wearily across the inns of the land until it didst come to pass that he could not get tick anywhere.

And in the fullness of time he didst repent his leaving of the land of Sullom, and didst return to his master, and didst throw himself at his feet crying, "Verily I beseech thee, O Lord, take thy errant sheep back into the fold."

And his master killeth not the fatted calf, but didst smite him hip and thigh and casteth him once more into the wilderness.

For it is writ: He that falleth from the gravy train will surely get a sore erse.